THE IDIOT GIRLS'
ACTION-ADVENTURE CLUB

THE IDIOT GIRLS' ACTION-ADVENTURE CLUB

Laurie Notaro

 VILLARD NEW YORK

All rights reserved under International and Pan-American Copyright Conventions.
Published in the United States by Villard Books, an imprint of The Random
House Publishing Group, a division of Random House, Inc., New York,
and simultaneously in Canada by Random House of
Canada Limited, Toronto.

VILLARD and V CIRCLED Design are registered trademarks of Random House, Inc.

Library of Congress Cataloging-in-Publication data is available.

ISBN 0-375-76091-1

Villard Books website address: www.villard.com
Printed in the United States of America

20 19 18 17 16 15 14 13 12

Book design by Carole Lowenstein

To Pop Pop, Douglas Hopkins, and Dick Vonier,
the best heroes a girl could have,
and Corbett Upton, who only seldomly complains
about playing the straight man

Contents

THE IDIOT GIRLS'
ACTION-ADVENTURE CLUB

Wrap & Roll and the Disappearance of Nikki's Keys

Nikki's keys were gone.

Just gone.

"I don't understand," I said emphatically. "You had them yesterday."

"I'm aware of that," she replied. "But somewhere in between being drunk yesterday and sober today, my keys vanished."

"And you're going to make me help you look for them, I suppose."

"No, you're going to *gladly* help me look for them because you're my friend and you also owe me forty dollars," she said.

Let me explain right now that Nikki does not do things in a small way, she never has. Take a simple thing like losing your keys. The last time she lost them, not only couldn't she drive anywhere, but she had also locked every door in the car for the first time in her life. This created a problem because she had left her roommate's dry cleaning in the trunk. And that created a problem because the dry cleaning consisted of every military uniform that he possessed. And that created another problem because he needed to be at the airport in two hours, since he was flying out on an Army mission overseas. And that created yet another problem, because he couldn't show up in civilian clothes at the Army place because he said they would immediately shoot him in the head or give him a dishonorable discharge, because the Army doesn't fire people, they just kill them or ruin their lives forever. And we still had yet another problem on our hands, and that was that Nikki was the only ride he had to the airport.

So, because Nikki lost her keys, someone was either going to die or spend the rest of his ruined life working at the only job he could get, which would probably be working at a record store or managing a record store. But the story actually didn't turn out too sad. After spending seventy-five dollars on a locksmith to get into the trunk, we found Nikki's keys, leisurely placed right smack on top of an arsenal of khaki-green uniforms.

And if the reconnaissance of Nikki's keys had a seventy-five-dollar price tag, there was a terrifying chance my forty-dollar loan might get called in, which was bad. Especially since it was most likely being deposited at that very moment in the bank account of our favorite bar.

"Please don't tell me that you were messing around with the trunk this time, or that your kid is sitting in the backseat with all of the windows rolled up, or that you left something of mine, like my CDs, on the front seat," I said as beads of worry were rolling down my forehead.

"I knew you'd help me! I just have to change into something yucky so I don't get dirty," she said before bounding up the stairs.

Whatever, I thought as I shook my head, and figured I'd get a head start by rifling through the cushions of the couch. I found a lighter right away, which I pocketed. Then I found thirty-seven cents, which I also pocketed, and a hairy LifeSaver that I left for the next couch-cushion bandit.

"Okay, I'm ready," she said as she came down the stairs, wearing the T-shirt with my caricature and name on the back that was made up during my days at Arizona State University's *State Press Magazine.*

"I thought you said you were going to put on something 'yucky,' " I said immediately. "That's my shirt. It's got my face on it. And my name. That's yucky? To you that's yucky?"

"I didn't mean *yucky* yucky, just, you know, yucky," she answered.

"So I'm not yucky yucky, I'm just plain yucky?" I snapped. "What would make it yucky yucky? Maybe if I had signed it or given it to you as a gift?"

"Yeah. No, I mean, it's my favorite shirt. I love this shirt," she explained.

"Well, I'm just sorry that it's so 'yucky.' I should have given you the ones we made out of the silk from those endangered worms."

She smiled. "Okay, I have to get my stick, and then we can go and look for my keys," she said.

"What do we need a stick for?" I asked. "We can break the car window with a rock."

"No, the stick isn't to break the window, it's to poke at the trash."

"We're poking at trash? Why are we poking at trash?" I asked.

"I think my keys are in the bottom of the trash bag that I took out yesterday."

"Let me get this straight: So you're wearing my shirt while we dig through other people's waste?"

"Right. See, if I thought it was yucky yucky, I'd wear it if the toilet overflowed."

Nikki found the stick—actually a broom handle—and we journeyed to the Dumpster, which is about as big as my house and smells worse. We climbed up the side and looked down into it, down into all of Nikki's trash as well as the trash of forty of her neighbors. That day, it was 114 degrees out, and the stench of the garbage was visible in stink lines that waved before my face in wiggly patterns, like in cartoons. Nikki started stabbing the trash with the stick, trying to find her own bag that was conveniently located at the very bottom.

Things were flying and falling everywhere—kitty litter and kitty turds, rotten vegetables and old food, used Kleenexes, and lots of dead things. Everybody in Nikki's complex is on birth control pills, I found out. All of a sudden, a bag Nikki had poked broke open, and then this little white thing rolled right in the center of my visual zone.

"AAAAAAAAAAAAHH!" I screamed.

"What?" Nikki asked as she started to turn toward me.

"Don't look!" I said as I blocked her view, knowing that she has a weak stomach and gets queasy when I talk about picking noses or when I mention anything whatsoever about poo, so I knew she would get sick if she saw what I saw, which was a white, naked, and, at some point, used tampon applicator.

Jesus, I thought to whomever it had belonged to, didn't your mother ever teach you about those things? I mean, Christ Almighty, as soon as my mother suspected that my ovaries were beginning to percolate, she sat me down in the only private room in the house—which was her bathroom—broke out a roll of toilet paper and a maxi pad, and taught me how to wrap & roll. Three wraps over the middle and three wraps over the side. Roll & wrap, it's the polite thing. Even I could figure it out at the age of eight. And, for added protection, you could stick God's little bundle in a plastic baggie, so when the dogs got loose in the house they wouldn't find it and tear it apart, as our dogs, Ginger and Brandy, loved to do. Immediately following the hands-on demonstration, I got the "Not-So-Fresh-Feeling" speech, after which I ran to my room and sobbed for an hour because Barbie didn't have an outfit that came with a tiny maxi pad, tampon, or Summer's Eve.

Well, we found Nikki's trash bag, but, of course, the keys weren't in it. In fact, as of this moment, Nikki lost her keys three weeks ago, and we still haven't found them. Who knows where they are?

Maybe, somehow, in the weird way that things work in Nikki's World, maybe someone wrapped Nikki's keys three times over the middle and three times over the side, and some hungry dog just ate them.

The Idiot Girls' Action-Adventure Club and the Art of Being Dumb

My friend Joel made an interesting point the other night.

"I'm happy that I'm one of the Dumb Ones," he informed me. "I like it better that way."

"Really?" I said. "Why?"

"Well, because there's stuff that I know about, and there's more stuff that I don't know about, which makes it less stuff that I have to worry about in the Big Picture," he answered.

He went on to explain further that his brother, Jeff, and our other friend, Jamie, were in the Smart Group, since they graduated from college and make more than $4.25 an hour. He also mentioned that from simply being around Jamie and Jeff, he could pick up pieces of intelligent information, which he calls "stories"—as in, say, who the vice president of the United States is or how to successfully pass a drug test. He, in turn, tells these stories to the people that he works with, who are also in the Dumb Group, and this makes Joel look Smart.

"I see," I replied. "So this makes you seem Smart, but you can still live an easier life as a Dumb One."

"Yep," he said. "See? I'm glad I was in retarded math in high school."

Then came the Question.

"Okay," I started. "If Jeff and Jamie are in the Smart Group, and you're in the Dumb Group, which one am I in?"

"Well," he sighed, "you're in the Dumb Group, too."

"Oh" was all I could say.

"But only because you're too cool to be in the Smart Group," he quickly added.

It was a nice save, I'll admit, but he was right. I had a feeling that I was in the Dumb Group, but I was never sure. And here I had it, on the opinion of an expert Dumb Person.

I should have known that, however, since I am a bona fide member of the Idiot Girls' Action-Adventure Club, which includes me and my friend Nikki and many of our other friends, including Krysti and Kate, all of whom are office-holding members.

I, of course, am the current elected president.

Hopefully, you'll recall that Nikki lost the keys to her car, and we couldn't find them. In fact, we never found them. Her car is still parked outside her apartment in the same forty-five-degree angle in which she parked it five weeks ago, only now it has two flat tires and has become a homestead of sorts to a band of feral cats and a crow.

Unfortunately for me, the story does not end there. Two weeks ago, while standing at her front door with a pint of whiskey surging through my bloodstream, she informed me that she had now lost her house key. It was okay, though, she slurred; we could still get in the house because her roommate had a crowbar in the trunk of her car, the keys to which Nikki *hadn't* lost yet.

I found out that night that being smashed does other things

to me besides making me believe that I am thin, attractive, and have a Motown-quality singing voice. It also makes me limber as a wrinkled prostitute, because I scaled a six-foot wall to Nikki's backyard in seconds flat, though the next day I woke up with so many bruises on my inner thighs that I thought I'd wrestled a gynecologist.

Booze can also give you superhuman strength, too, and I saw that with my own eyes, as Nikki took the crowbar to the back door. With one pry, the door flew open, and part of the metal door jamb rocketed fifteen feet up into the night air. We were in the house. We smiled. We thought we were Smart.

Then we realized that the frame was so badly bent and so many pieces of it were missing that the door was rendered unlockable. Now we realized that we were Dumb, especially when our friend Mike came over and laughed at us because we had tried to disillusion potential burglars by making our own lock with a piece of rope and some tape and it fell off the door when he touched it.

I've been Dumb tons of other times, too, like when I tried to spite the postman by leaving all of the junk mail in the mailbox because I was just sick and tired of throwing it away. I left it there for four weeks until he finally took it back, and I had won. I was Smart. Then he quit delivering mail to me and left me a nasty note declaring my house a vacant residence. Then I was Dumb.

I was at the bar and spotted an incredibly cute boy with long, blond hair across the room. I smiled, and he smiled back. I started acting cute, sucking in my stomach and sending him alluring looks, and he kept staring at me. I was being Smart. I moved to the middle of the room, kept on acting cute, messing with my hair and stuff, and moved in even closer. I was pretty close—like, on the bar stool next to him—when I realized that he knew exactly all the girl things I was doing, because "he" was a girl himself. And she was prettier than me. Then I was Dumb.

I was Very Dumb when my ex-boyfriend, the Super Demon Brad, broke up with me. He didn't actually break up with me, however; the Super Demon Brad simply intended to move out of the state with his gauze-wearing, cornrow-haired ex-girlfriend, Dog Girl, without telling me. I found this out when I went to his apartment one day, and he was packing all of his stuff into a piece-of-shit hippie van with purple curtains. Purple curtains! It was then that he told me that he felt his true direction in life was to follow the Grateful Dead. Dog Girl had bought a van, sewed up the curtains, and he was leaving. And he did.

I was Dumb when I didn't fish out the fork I had in my purse, and I was Dumber when I didn't stab him and her in the throat with it. Instead, I thought I was being Smart by turning around and walking away without saying a word, though he kept on insisting that I should hit him. If I had the chance now, I'd rip his teeth out with my bare hands and weave them into Dog Girl's braids. Instead, I hopped on a plane the next morning to Portland, Oregon, where my runner-up boyfriend picked me up at the airport.

Anyway, because I am Dumb, and an Idiot Girl, not only do I have memories of the stupid things I've done, I also have pictures, since that's what happens when a Dumb One gets control of a camera. During a recent Idiot Girls Adventure in which myself, Nikki, and Idiot Girls' Club treasurer, Kate, drove up north to Flagstaff to check out the Nude Olympics, I brought along a camera to pictorialize the fine event. When we finally got up north, however, we couldn't find any naked people, even though there were apparently hundreds of them strutting around.

We took a wrong turn and got lost on some backwoods dirt road that we kept driving on until someone said they had to pee. We stopped the car, found a couple of used tissues, and headed off into the woods. That was when one of the other two Idiots decided that this was something we needed photographs of, and we weren't even drunk. Now, thanks to the trigger-happy finger of one very avid photographer, there are several items of evidence in existence that show me in various stages of talking to a man about a horse, pulling down my pants, wiping—and then hurriedly pulling up my pants when I realized that someone was watching me. It's okay though, when I got the pictures I really didn't mind. Whoever took the pictures was too Dumb to realize that they were too far away, and all you can really see is something that looks like Bigfoot playing with his private parts, even though Bigfoot has been Smart enough not to let someone snap an image of him peeing in the dirt.

All I could do was laugh. After all, that's what the Dumb Ones do best.

Ashes to Ashes, Bones to Dust, My Mother Always Said Underwear Is a Must

The box sat on the kitchen counter, wrapped in green foil Christmas paper. I knew it was for me. I was at my mother's house and no one in my family was speaking to me because I showed up an hour late for my birthday dinner and they were mad since they knew it was the one time that they couldn't start eating without me.

I shook the box and instantly knew what it was, although I hoped I was wrong. It was related to my "condition."

I'm too young and not mature enough to have this condition, I'll tell you that right now. I'm not ready for it, it has sharply bitten a chunk out of my social life, and it's going to stick around for the rest of my natural existence, I'm sure. For those of you do-gooder, nosy, can't-mind-your-own-damn-business types who are already flipping through the white pages searching for the telephone number to Child Protective Services, rest easy. I'm not pregnant. I'm just crippled by agonizing back pain.

My spine is slowly, though not quietly, turning to dust, and I can't believe it. I always figured it would be my lungs that jumped ship first, followed a foot behind by my liver. It made me happy to picture myself in an iron lung or an oxygen tent, turning up my artificial voice box to full blast and screaming at the nurses to get me a cigarette, goddamnit! My dreams have burst like an artery in my head—where is the justice in this? I just never pictured myself zooming around the aisles of Fry's liquor warehouse in a motorized Rascal with a metal basket on the front, asking a clerk to toss me the jumbo Tampax variety pack because it's on the top shelf and I can't reach it. And can you get a DUI while operating an electric wheelchair?

I've been to the chiropractor, and he shot me in the head and in the butt with this metal gun thing. Then he put a wet, vibrating tube on my back, and when I told the boys at work about this, they all said they'd do the same thing to me, but for free.

The pain was incredible, and sure, the booze helped for a while, but eventually that comfort evaporated. I knew I had to find a medical expert with experience and credentials, as well as the ability to get me some good drugs. I was off to the bone specialist.

My mother had to go with me because I couldn't drive, I could barely stand up. She went into the examining room with me, where the nurse told me to disrobe and then put on a paper gown that made me look like my aunt who has a drinking problem and couldn't wear pants for six months after being maimed in a bizarre baking accident. Apparently, flour and gin do not mix. The nurse told me I could leave my tights on if I got cold, and I thought this was a good idea because I wasn't wearing any underwear. You know why. My dogs kept eating them, so I quit buying them.

I was sitting on the examining table thing; my mother was on a little chair perpendicular to the table. She gasped when I took off my boot.

"Look at the hole in your tights!" she said, pointing to my foot. It actually wasn't a hole, however; it started out as a hole on my big toe and then grew big enough to strangle the big toe, so one night under the influence I got angry, kicked off the boot, and killed the hole, ripping the entire foot of the tights off.

"I can't believe you wore those tights to the doctor's office!" she insisted, shaking her head. "I am so embarrassed. Aren't you embarrassed? You ought to be embarrassed. I'm embarrassed just looking at you. A homeless person wouldn't even wear those tights to a doctor's office, they'd be so embarrassed. Good God, is this the way I raised you? That doctor's going to think you're indigent!"

Finally, during my mother's ranting and raving, Dr. Bone Specialist came in, made me stand up and hobble across the room, checked my reflexes, and then made me lie down on the table. He bent my right leg this way and that way, up and down, all the way out to the side and in. Then he did the same with my left leg. He ordered X rays, then started to leave the room. I panicked. I MUST GET DRUGS.

"What can I take for the pain?" I asked him before he got out the door.

"You can take some over-the-counter ibuprofen," he suggested. "But I wouldn't take more than nine a day."

I choked. Nine a day? I'd been popping *forty*. Nine a day? *Like hell.* I couldn't even go to the bathroom on my own, I hadn't slept in three weeks, and my normally sunny, cheery disposition had turned into that of a very rabid dog. If I didn't get good drugs and get them *now*, it was straight to Shooter's World and then Walgreens pharmacy for me.

"I don't think you understand," I explained. "I can't go to work. I have spent the last four days with my mother, who is addicted to QVC, watching jewelry shows, doll shows, and make-up shows. I almost ordered a beef-jerky maker! Give me something, *or I'm going to use your calf muscles to make the first batch!*"

Without any further ado, he hastily scribbled out a prescription for some codeine and was gone. I was happy.

My mother, however, had lost the ability to speak. She had a hollow look on her face that I hadn't expected to see until she traveled way past menopause on the road map of life. She would be living with me, and I would get to put bows in her hair, pay her a dime for emptying out the dishwasher, dress her up in little pink polyester sweaters, and make her eat at the kids' table on holidays.

"You have a hole in your tights," she mumbled.

"I know, Mom, we've already been through the disgrace of my naked foot," I sighed.

"Not *there!*" she hissed, barely audible. "Not there! HERE!" She began pointing to her private parts again and again, unable to stop—"HERE! THE HOLE IS HERE!"—until for a brief moment she made a circle with her thumbs and index fingers, extended to the size of a ripe honeydew melon. "This big," she said. "This damn big. And that doctor saw it! Why the hell aren't you wearing underwear?"

I had flashed my doctor. As well as my mother. I had made

myself more genitally and visibly available than anyone that graced the pages of Hustler. And I wasn't even being paid for it.

So I know what is in this box that's sitting on the kitchen counter, the contents of which my sister has carefully picked out and wrapped for me.

I opened it, dug through the tissue paper, and there they were: six pairs of white cotton briefs from Sears, so large they could have doubled for car covers. I imagined myself in them, the waistband resting just underneath my breasts, looking a lot like if Gene Hackman were to model for Hanes.

"Why, thank you," I said to my sister. "I saw these in the Victoria's Secret catalog. The woman who was wearing them also had on a colostomy bag and was pushing a walker."

"They'll shrink if you wash them," she offered.

"To what?" I answered. "The size of a hot-air balloon? Nuns don't even wear underwear like this."

"Nuns don't go around exposing their who-see-whats-its to unsuspecting doctors," my mother chimed in.

Then she made my other sister go upstairs and get all of her old underwear in case I had to go to the doctor more than six times.

The panty war was over. I had lost.

My mother smiled. She thought she had won.

She's not the real winner, though. The real winners of the underwear war are placed strategically at their bowls of Sunshine Chunks in my kitchen right now, waiting patiently and craftily for their opportunity to claim, and then eat, the victory prize.

The Good, the Bad, and the Ugly

Goddamnit, I've never been "the pretty friend."

The Pretty Friend. Shudder. Shiver. Smash.

She's the one who wears the perfect eyeliner, it never gathers like a crowd in her tear ducts to create a grapefruit-size ebony eye booger.

The one who can wear a bodysuit, sit down in it, and not have rolls of fat cascading over her belt.

The one who can eat a sandwich or hamburger and not wind up with lipstick on the bun or on her chin.

The one who can actually eat in front of other people and not have food, like coleslaw, hanging from her lip or shooting out of her mouth, landing on the plates of other diners.

She never spits when she talks.

She sleeps with her mouth shut and never drools.

She doesn't pick at her face.

And she never, ever has to take a shit.

I carry a book of matches wherever I go, just in case, because I'm regular. Very regular. Sometimes at night, I slobber so much when I sleep that my hair is still wet the next morning. I have never lived a day in my life when I didn't spend a good majority of it with lipstick on my teeth. In fact, I estimate that I probably ingest the equivalent of eight tubes of lipstick a year. I often forget to wear deodorant and then have to sniff at my own armpits to check if I've remembered personal hygiene that day. When people ask me how many cigarettes I smoke in a day, I answer with, "I don't know. Smell my hair and you tell me." I haven't worn a bodysuit or a shirt tucked in since I was in the third grade. And no one, I mean no one, has ever seen me naked with the lights on.

But I'm not sure this is my fault.

Pretty friends always have cute names, like Nicole, Colleen, Dionne, or Jamie. So I figure this pretty-friend thing has to start fairly early, like when you're born and named. That decides it right there. My mother did a better job naming her dogs, Cali and Cory, than she did me, Laurie Ann, and I have to live longer. I can't even shorten my name to something like Lauri; I would just end up making myself plural. There you go. It was set in stone in 1965. I was destined to be the Ugly Friend; the nurses looked at me in that bassinet and sadly shook their heads.

"The poor thing, that Laurie Ann," one nurse said. "She was decent-looking when she first came in as 'Baby Girl Notaro,' but look at her now. That thing just sprouted thick black hair on her toes."

"Ugh, gives me the shivers," the other nurse replied. "Look at how her pores are expanding. Is that a boil or a goiter on her chin? When she grows up, I'll bet money that she snorts when she laughs and can eat three pounds of pork products in one sitting."

"I'll bet she'll be a loud-mouthed drunk," the first nurse

added. "Let's move her to that dark corner away from the pretty babies, Molly and Michelle. We don't want her to ruin them."

The Ugly Friends never get the attention that their Pretty Friends get. No boys ever want to know where the Ugly Friends are (at the Ugly Friends' Clubhouse, of course, where we watch endless episodes of *The Golden Girls*, eat troughs of cheesecake, and then try on girdles), but the boys will always ask the Ugly Friends, "Hey, where's your Pretty Friend ————?" to which I always want to answer, "In the hospital having some additional plastic surgery. Don't tell me you thought that perky nose was real?"

In fact, it's the Ugly Friends that always wind up playing in-terference for the Pretty Friends when a slimy man-creature takes a fancy to the friend who hasn't rubbed away the inner thighs of every damn pair of pants she owns.

I remember one night out at a bar when I was with Nikki, my Pretty Friend. A Man-Beast kept chasing her around the bar, grappling at her butt, which, unlike mine, could not double as a sectional sofa that could comfortably accommodate a family of five. This went on for hours—grab, grab, grab, feel, feel, feel—until finally I turned around and took hold of the bas-tard's arm.

I knew what I had to do. I had to protect my friend, and I had to do it in a way that the Man-Beast would understand. I had to pretend to be Nikki's significant other, and, being the uglier of the two, I had to be the dominant one, the Husband lesbian. (The Ugly Friends never get to be the Wife lesbian, they always have to be the mister.)

"Listen, you man," I said with disdain, tightening my grip. "That's my baby you're messing with, and if you touch her one more time, it's going to be you and me in that back alley, throwing blows."

An Ugly Woman never lies. She doesn't have to. I was wearing flannel. The Man-Beast cowered backward and never touched Nikki again.

Unfortunately, a confrontation is the only true way that an Ugly Friend really knows how to deal with a man without making it obvious that she is a complete loser. A Pretty Friend can't teach her, and it really doesn't matter, because as soon as the Ugly Friend hooks herself a man, he will immediately become enamored with the Pretty Friend the moment he lays eyes on her majestic beauty, anyway.

The Pretty Friends know how to charm a man, let the man know that, yes, they are a woman. The Ugly Friends don't have a virgin's chance in hell. For instance, I know that I like a man as soon as I sucker punch him in the gut or vomit in front of him—most likely getting some of the disgorge on him. There's no charm involved here.

My great friend Krysti was once hanging out with her Pretty Friend Kim, when she decided to impress a man she liked. She was smoking, of course, because you can't be my friend if you don't smoke, and chose to flick the butt of her cigarette in a very cool fashion to let the man know that she was a sexy, right-on chick.

Krysti is normally very good at this and can flick her butt to unnatural and awe-inspiring distances, much farther than either one of us can spit. I've seen her do it. In this instance, however, the butt propelled through the air in a slight, delicate arc and hit the man of desire square in the crotch. It lodged itself like a magnet in between two inconspicuous folds of material and still, miraculously, remained lit.

Sensing imminent danger, Krysti immediately swatted at the man's genital region to save his member from the burning ash, though he only understood this maneuver to be a spontaneous, sexually expressive act.

Kim, of course, was no help. She still looked foxy rolling around on the ground, laughing like a Pretty Friend does, with tears streaming out of her eyes. Her mascara, naturally, did not run.

Krysti was left alone to explain to the ex-potential suitor that she had lunged for his penis only because it was easier than knocking him down and rolling him in the dirt once he burst into flames.

And as Krysti told me this story, I understood why I would never be the Pretty Friend. It was evident in my laugh, as soon as the pig snort escaped when I tried to take a breath. It was a *Hee Haw*, barnyard-donkey snort, one that sucked in all the mucus from my nasal cavity and shoved it in a river down my throat, causing me to cough so hard that I puked right then and there in the bathroom sink.

What a waste, I thought, all of that perfectly good vomit.

It just might have been worthwhile if there had been a man around.

Aw, hell. If a man *had* been around, he would have looked at the puddle of puke, leaned down to wipe it off his shoes, and then, quickly and politely, asked for Nikki's phone number.

Suckers

It was 1976.

I remember the orientation in sixth grade when the boys went with the gym coach and the girls went with the school nurse into separate rooms and learned about male and female private parts and how to spawn. It was one of the darkest days of my life when that nurse, Mrs. Shimmer, pulled out a maxi pad that measured the width and depth of a mattress and showed us how to use it. It had a belt with it that looked like a slingshot that possessed the jaw-dropping potential to pop a man's head like a gourd. As she stretched the belt between the fingers of her two hands, Mrs. Shimmer told us that becoming a woman was a magical and beautiful thing.

I remember thinking to myself, You're damn right it had better be magic, because that's going to be what it takes to get me to wear something like that, Tinkerbell! It looked like a saddle. Weighed as much as one, too. Some girls even cried.

I didn't.

I raised my hand.

"Mrs. Shimmer," I asked the nurse cautiously, "so what kind of security napkins do *boys* wear when their flower pollinates? Does it have a belt, too?"

The room got quiet except for a bubbling round of giggles.

"You haven't been paying attention, have you?" Mrs. Shimmer accused sharply. "Boys have stamens, and stamens do not require sanitary napkins. They require self-control, but you'll learn that soon enough."

I was certainly hoping that my naughty bits (what Mrs. Shimmer explained to us was like a pistil of a flower) didn't get out of control, because I had no idea what to do if they did. Maybe that's why Mrs. Shimmer said that girls should stay away from horseback riding when it was "their time." I could see how a horse could really get spooked with a wild and whipping pistil coming at them, wagging like a cobra with an appetite for death.

"And stay out of the water!" she added. "No swimming, especially in oceans! You could easily pollute a public pool, and if you even set foot in the ocean, fish from miles around will pick up the scent!"

She then reiterated the perils of becoming a woman by displaying on an easel a poem about the subject, which replaced her hand-drawn diagram of a bleeding flower that bore the title "You're in Bloom!" She had apparently penned the poem herself, which she made us read together out loud.

"Menstruation,
Fact of life;
Belts and pads
From girl to wife.

> Though cramps and spotting
> May keep you down,
> You're now a queen
> With Kotex as crown.
>
> Swimming's out,
> Just stay inside.
> Sharks can tell,
> So keep it dry!"

The whole thing, frankly, was freaking me out.

"But my mom doesn't use a belt," my best friend Jamie said from where she sat beside me. "Her maxi pads have a sticky strip."

Mrs. Shimmer whipped around, and her happy-poem face melted into one of sinister, thrashing contempt.

"Practice using the belt!" she shot, her glare directed straight at the corner where Jamie and I sat on wooden benches in the PE dressing room. "Sticky strips are a fad! Nothing replaces the security of a belt! Nothing!"

I got the feeling that Mrs. Shimmer didn't really like being a girl. She didn't really feel like a queen when she pinned that belt into place, I could tell. It wasn't magic to her. Not even a card trick.

None of the eleven-year-olds in that room had a look that said something magical or beautiful was about to happen to her. We wanted to ride horses, we wanted to go swimming, we wanted to use sticky strips when the time came. No one wanted to strap a slingshot around her private parts to keep the pistil restrained. Every single one of us had a look on her face that said we had all been duped.

Like we were all suckers.

It Smells Like Doody Here

Every August, a couple of weeks before school started, my father would crank the handle on our pop-up trailer and air it out in our carport.

It was the sole signal that it was time for another Notaro family vacation, and a sign that in the coming weeks ahead, our family would return from some spot up north, traumatized, most likely injured, and suffering from post-traumatic stress disorder.

None of us, to this day, knows why my dad bought the trailer. I was ten when he came home one Saturday afternoon with it hitched to the bumper of the Country Squire station wagon, swaying and groaning as it pulled into the driveway.

"We're going camping!" my father said.

My sisters and I nodded. Then we went back inside and fought with one another.

At first, my father would chart our camping journey, studying maps and marking lakes and campsites. Well, they really weren't campsites but KOAs, which are basically big paved parking lots off the sides of highways, with spigots and maybe a gift shop. There really wasn't much for me and my sisters to do for an entire week except find rocks and try to sell them to one another, or bug my mom for a quarter so we could buy Jolly Rancher candies from the gift shop and then loiter. One gift shop lady got so aggravated with our frequent visits that she wanted to talk to our mom. When we explained that Mom was lying down with her hand on her head because she got a headache when we got there on Saturday, the gift shop lady just made us promise not to come back again. So we went back to the trailer and fought with one another for the next four days.

When I was in eighth grade, my dad finally broke free from the safety of the KOAs and decided that we were experienced enough to try a real campsite, one with dirt. He had heard of a great spot in the White Mountains, near a lake. He aired out the trailer in the carport, and the next week we were on our way.

When we got there, Dad found a great spot right by the lake and parked the trailer.

"It smells like doody here," my youngest sister said.

"It does not," my mother snapped. "That's the way lakes smell."

We popped the trailer up and brought in our pillows and sleeping bags from the car. As soon as my mom brought over the last bag of food, the sky broke open, and it started to rain.

Then it started to pour.

And then it started to hail.

"It'll stop soon," my dad said.

"I have to go to the bathroom," my other sister said quietly.

We all looked at each other. The toilet was in the trailer, yes, but its location was not in what you would call a discreet spot. It was, in fact, under the cushion that acted as a bench on one side of the table, which also turned into a bed at night.

"Now?" my mother said. "You have to go now?"

My sister nodded. My mother took the groceries off the tabletop, my father dismantled it, and the cushion was lifted.

"Go ahead," my mother said, motioning.

"Make them go outside," my sister insisted.

"I'm totally not going outside," I said irritably. "Forget you! For sure! Dream on!"

"Everybody out," my father demanded, and we stood in the downpour to give my sister some privacy.

"This is getting ridiculous!" my mother said after ten minutes, as she knocked on the door, her cigarette wet and broken in half. "All right already!"

My sister opened the door and returned to her spot on one of the beds, where she wasn't doing anything but reading People magazine.

After standing in four inches of water and mud, our shoes were soaked through, and my mom wouldn't let us in the trailer until we took them off.

"From now on," she said, pointing a finger at all of us, "if you have to go to the bathroom, hold up a towel around you!"

My father gathered up all of our wet shoes from outside and took our small hibachi out under a tree. After lighting a fire and watching it carefully, he placed our sneakers on the grill until he was satisfied they were dry. He was getting ready to bring the shoes back into the trailer when he realized the soles had melted so thoroughly that they had become one with the hibachi. He entered the trailer with the sentence, "I hope you guys brought a lot of socks."

For the next six days, we were confined to the trailer while the rain continued to pour down around us in sheets, all of us shoeless except for my sister. She read her *People* magazine over and over while my remaining sister and I fought. My father stared out the window looking at the rain, and my mother lay on the bed with her hand over her head.

It was on that sixth day that my mother begged my father to get us out of there. "I can't stand it anymore!" she pleaded. "I took the last of the Tylenol this morning!"

My father explained that we were in the mountains, on an inclined dirt road that had by now seen a foot of rain. It was impossible, he said from behind the held-up towel; it would be too dangerous.

"Then *you* just go see how the roads are," she said adamantly. "I'm also out of cigarettes, you know!"

My father got the keys to the Country Squire and headed out. "Get the kids a board game before I kill us all!" she shouted as he pulled away.

"And this week's *People*!" my sister yelled.

He returned twenty minutes later, empty-handed and frustrated. The road was too muddy, he said. We'd just have to wait it out.

Later that night, as I was sleeping on the toilet bed, my head over the bowl, I was awakened by a jostle. As I sat up, I felt the trailer move slightly, then move again. Another, more violent, jolt was the one that woke the rest of my family.

"What is it?" my sister yelled.

"It smells like doody!" my other sister cried.

Another bump. I started to get really scared. Oh my god, it's Bigfoot, I thought, sucking myself into a white, blinding panic. "It is so totally Bigfoot!"

We heard movement around the trailer. To the right. To the left. In front. In back.

"Dad?" my youngest sister asked. "Is a bear going to eat us?"

"Jesus, Mary, and Joseph, it's a bear!" my mother yelled. "It's a bear! Run!"

"We don't have any shoes!" my youngest sister screamed.

"It's Sasquatch!" I heard myself yell. "It's the yeti! Talk to it softly, and we'll be okay!"

"Whoever has my *People* magazine," my other sister said sharply, "I did not give you my permission to read it!"

My father, in the midst of the chaos, had made it to the trailer door and was peeking out the window. We didn't notice as he opened the door and stood there, watching.

Cows. Lots and lots of cows. A herd of them surrounded the trailer as they moved through the campsite and on to the other side of the lake, bumping into our trailer as they clumsily made their way along. We, apparently, had camped in their pasture. It did smell like doody.

My dad paid a guy with a Chevy truck thirty bucks and the *People* magazine to tow us out the next morning to the main road and to give my mom a cigarette.

We all had nightmares for weeks.

The next year, when he cranked up the trailer, my mom came out of the house, shot him a look, then lay down on her bed with her hand on her head.

He sold it the following week.

A Morsel from the Garden of Eden

The basket had been passed, and there was no way out of it.

It was my turn.

Ever since my grandfather, Pop Pop, had gotten sick, my mother, two sisters, and an uncle all had our turns. We worked in shifts, and duty generally called us in once a week.

I never knew what my assignment with Pop Pop was until I got to his and Nana's house. It was like flipping a coin, though usually it consisted of one of three things: taking Pop Pop to the bank, to the bakery, or, the most feared of all the duties, to the grocery store.

Pop Pop had been on medication to relieve some of the pain that the cancer had caused, which worked really well; in fact it worked so well that I briefly thought of "borrowing" some. In turn, this mother of all painkillers had made him slightly dizzy and more forgetful than usual, so his nurses assured us that it was in his best interest not to drive. Actually, they assured us that it was in the general population of Phoenix's best interest that he not so much as commandeer a shopping cart on anything that could even slightly be considered pavement.

So here and there, whenever he expressed a need to go somewhere, he would make Nana call one of us up and arrange to take him to his destination. He usually expressed his need by yelling that he had become "a caged animal" and that he felt he was an "inmate in his own home." This, coupled with the fact that he'd insisted for fifty years that Nana never needed to learn how to drive, is how we began taking turns, although he did begin spreading the rumor that he was going to get himself an electric wheelchair so he could take himself to Safeway—which was three miles away and a quick hop over an interstate from his house.

It was revealed that Pop Pop was ignoring his nurses' advice and had been driving himself around the neighborhood to run his errands. We discovered this when my younger sister went to visit and saw that one of the posts supporting the green carport was now standing at a sixty-degree angle, in addition to the suspicion that one side of his car had been visibly sideswiped by something big and wooden and green. When confronted with the evidence, Pop Pop insisted with a huge grin that he was simply "reparking" his car and hadn't even driven out into the street, although Nana stood behind him and continually rolled her eyes.

In any case, taking Pop Pop to the grocery store was always the least desirable turn, especially since that's where his area of expertise bloomed. He had been a grocer since the days of the Depression, and felt that he had learned a couple of things in his time, which he wanted to pass on to the next generation of grocers. This included sometimes verbally assaulting butchers, cashiers, bakers, and general managers, though he usually left the bag boys alone. Everyone in every store knew him by his name and knew him on sight—evident by the way they suddenly disappeared upon catching a glimpse of him shuffling down the aisles.

When I got to my grandparents' house on the day of my turn, Pop Pop already had his coupons and his strategy laid out. We were going, undoubtedly, to the grocery store.

As he gathered his store advertisements and got his cane, he looked at me and disgustedly shook his head.

"You know, Laur," he said, grimacing, "I've been praying to God for three days for something to feed the birds, and not one time this week have I found anything on the day-old racks. What am I going to do? What the hell am I supposed to do?"

"Don't you bring any old bread home, Nick!" my Nana shouted from the kitchen. "I just got rid of all the goddamned ants in the backyard from the last moldy loaf you spread around out there."

"Ah, Christ," Pop Pop said to me, shaking his head again, "I am a caged animal. A goddamned caged animal in my own house."

I decided not to say anything.

"I hope we find some old bread," he continued as I held his cane and helped him into the car. "Sometimes they throw the old bread away."

Oh, no. I was having no part of this. No sir.

"You can forget it, Pop, I'm not getting in the Dumpster," I said firmly. "I don't care if the voice of the Lord was commanding me from a fiery Hefty bag, it's not going to happen."

Pop Pop looked at me in complete disgust. "You don't have to get in," he asserted. "Most of the time you don't have to dig that much; they put the bread right on top."

I hoped that I was doing a poor job at evaluating the situation as I drove him to Safeway and followed his directions to pull into the loading docks behind the store, where a Boar's Head truck was already parked and being unloaded.

"There's the Dumpster," Pop Pop said, pointing. "Just stop right here."

I stopped the car and didn't even have time to turn off the engine when I heard Pop Pop gasp. I looked up. I couldn't believe what I saw.

It was Pop Pop's Holy Grail.

His pot of gold.

A morsel from the Garden of Eden.

It was a shopping cart, directly in front of us as if God had placed it there himself, nearly toppling over with bakery goods.

I will swear on anything that the eighty-two-year-old man in the seat next to me, who was using a cane merely nine minutes before, got out of that car and ran to the cart.

He dragged it back to the car, flung open the back door, and began shoveling the equivalent of a Hostess warehouse into my backseat.

There were brownies and cheesecakes and jelly rolls. There were loaves of bread and poppy-seed rolls and hot dog buns. There were Oreo layer cakes and lemon loaves and something that had peanut butter in it.

"I can't believe it, I can't believe it," Pop Pop kept saying. "Most of this stuff is only one day past code! One day!"

I wouldn't have believed it either if I hadn't seen it firsthand. After eighty-two years, he had finally done it.

Pop Pop had won the lottery.

The backseat was nearly full when I heard a loud beeping sound, and Pop Pop began screaming.

"Oh my God! Laurie! The Boar's Head truck! The Boar's Head truck!"

And then I saw it; the big red-and-black truck with the pig's head on the side was backing up quickly, and was in danger of very quickly driving over my car.

What else could I do? I hit the gas. I had to. If I get in one more car accident, my insurance gets revoked. I had only driven a couple of feet, only enough to escape danger. But I guess a couple of feet was all it took to drag my grandfather—who despite the mortal severity of the situation could not interrupt his heist for two to three seconds—almost to the ground.

I gasped when I saw him get knocked over by the car, but he got right back up and tossed another cheesecake into the backseat.

"Are you all right?" I screamed at him.

"I can't stop, gotta keep loading," he assured me. "Gotta keep loading!"

My mom was going to kill me when I told her that I had run Pop Pop over with the car. It would prove how irresponsible I was. I couldn't even take an old man to Safeway without hurting him and giving him road rash.

Finally, when the entire backseat was so full that it was filled up nearly to the roof, Pop Pop got back in the car with a look of a man twenty years younger.

"See?" he affirmed. "I told you! I told you! I prayed to God for bread, and he answered my prayers!"

"But I ran you over and almost killed you because of the bread," I replied.

"Eh," he sighed, "what the hell's a little dirt?"

I nodded. "Yeah," I agreed, "but you better start praying again, and you better pray harder this time. Because when Nana sees what's in the backseat, she's going to kick your ass."

He just looked at me and laughed.

The Useless Black Bra and the Stinkin'-Drunk Twelve-Step Program

Joel and I had driven down Eighty-sixth Street five times in succession. We were looking for Jeff and Jamie, our friends who we were supposed to follow and pick up after the Tally Ho, our favorite bar, had closed.

They had left ten minutes before us, since both had decided to walk the half-mile back to Jeff's house because they were so smashed that there was no way that either one of them could find the street, let alone drive their cars.

Now they were nowhere in sight.

Jamie had quit drinking a year ago to avoid all of the extremely embarrassing things she had done in public when her alter personality, Otis Campbell, took over. Tonight, Otis was back with a vengeance, his presence evident after she drank her first five beers. Before she had even set foot in the Tally Ho, her eyes had rolled back in her head, and she had already fallen out of her shoes a couple of times. We saw her grasping for the jukebox for stability as she swayed back and forth, trying hard to focus on something, plugging in quarters to play her favorite Gin Blossoms song, "Hey Jealousy."

As she hummed along, she explained to Joel that she had a

Psychic Pregnancy lighter. If it lit, she was pregnant. If it only sparked, she wasn't. She flicked the lighter, and it sparked.

"My boyfriend doesn't think he's fertile," she slurred, her eyes crossing. "But I tell him, 'Shooting blanks makes just as much noise, baby.' "

Even I gasped.

But now, at 1:30 A.M., we couldn't find her or Jeff.

"At what point do we abandon the search and go home to finish getting drunk?" Joel wanted to know, since he had become quite tired of the whole escapade.

In a matter of three minutes, however, Joel was going to understand that a drunk girl is never a pretty girl, even if her condition begs for the click of a camera. It was definitely worth his wait.

There is a series of steps that a drinker takes to reach the pedestal of Stinkin' Drunk, a chronological collection of actions that take place in order to fully guarantee that they will achieve the Full Fun Potential of the night.

Fun-and-Frolic Jamie has graduated from this school with honors.

THE STINKIN'-DRUNK TWELVE-STEP PROGRAM

Step One: The Call of the Drink

It beckons to you, you simply answer it. It sounds like a good idea, it feels right, but you decide you will not go too far.

Step Two: Economics

If funds are low, and you don't have an entire paycheck to blow, you must decide whether to do the Poor Man's Drunk (i.e., drinking on a completely empty stomach) or if there is some possibility that you can con others into providing for you.

Step Three: The Suitable Drinking Partner

Finding the appropriate person may sometimes prove a little difficult, but a sensible choice has no substitute. You must be careful not to choose a beginner, because you will inevitably end up taking care of them and wiping up body fluids, but you also must be careful not to choose someone who will be functioning well enough when you pass out to stick hot dogs down your pants or cement your eyes shut with toothpaste.

Step Four: The Clink of the Ice, the Crack of the Tab

The first sip that holds beautiful promises, the initial lick of the lips that christens the inebriation that lies patiently ahead. The drinker begins to feel at ease, shedding the sober skin in thicker flakes after each and every drink.

(The next eight steps can follow in rapid succession or may occur simultaneously.)

Step Five: Sad Reminiscing

"I don't care if I saw him naked on the couch with that girl who works at Dairy Queen, I know he really loved me. Why did he leave me? Why? Can anyone tell me why?" The most worthless step of the entire twelve. It usually concerns relationships and can lead to potentially hazardous DWIs—Dialing While Intoxicated—which entails calling everyone you ever dated, since you are convinced that it is a completely excellent idea.

Step Six: Wanting to Get Naked and Asking Strangers to Do the Same

Usually done after the DWI has already taken place, and the drinker has been rejected again.

Step Seven: Math

You start figuring out how many hours it will be until you have to be fully functioning again. "I can sleep fifteen more minutes if I skip a shower," "I'll wear what I'm wearing now and won't have to waste time looking for something clean."

Step Eight: "It's Ten 'til One" Inventory

A quick assessment that no matter how much liquor you have, it will not be enough and you must get more, and NOW, because it is the most important mission you will ever embark on in your life.

Step Nine: Let's Get a Snack, Too

A journey to a drive-thru, because you are much too drunk to sit in a restaurant, though you are okay to drive. Purchase twenty dollars' worth of fast food that will most likely reappear in an altogether different form before sunrise. You will eat things at this point that you would not normally feed your dog, like convenience-store franks or three-for-a-dollar tacos.

Step Ten: I Love Being Me

You are witty. You begin feeling beautiful, sexy, and thin. You *really* want to be naked now, and just about everybody is looking good. You will not think twice about sticking your tongue down a stranger's throat in a room full of a hundred people. You may also feel the need to tell assorted people that you love them, and this is a good indication that you should probably go home.

Step Eleven: Invisibility

You believe that you are invisible and can do things that will bear no witnesses, like peeing in a bush or puking on the sidewalk. It is at this point that you will not remember the last thing you said or that you decided that the street looks like a very good place to lie down.

Step Twelve: The Complete Loop

You lose the ability to communicate, with the exception of nodding your head. Also evaporated is the decision-making process, all of your money, the use of your limbs, and, quite thankfully, consciousness.

When we finally found Jeff sitting in the street, he had successfully arrived at step ten.

"We were hiding from you," he giggled as he got in the car. "We saw you drive down the street five times. Aren't we good at hiding?"

I was mad. "Where is the other half of the Moron Twins?" I asked.

"I don't know," he offered. "I lost her."

"You lost Jamie?"

"Yeah. She thought this was my street and started running, sort of. She was falling down a lot," he said. "I don't think we'll find her. I bet she's still hiding."

I drove up the street. I drove down the street. We couldn't find her. We drove around the neighborhood for forty-five minutes, checking behind shrubs, fences, and cars, following leads from various people on the street who had seen a drunk girl stumbling down the road in several different directions.

We drove back down the street where Jeff had lost her, each of us searching a side of the road.

"Stop," Joel said dryly. "There she is. She'd probably better put her shirt on, though. 'Hey Jealousy.' "

I thought he was kidding. I prayed that he was kidding. But as I got out of the car and walked toward Joel's side of the street, I saw Jamie, lying like a corpse in someone's front yard, a desert landscape, topless. The only thing she had on above her waist was a black bra, which wasn't doing her a whole lot of good anyway.

"I remember now," Jeff said. "She kept saying that she was hot."

Since Jamie had drunk her weight in beer and resembled a sandbag with arms and legs, it took the three of us to lift the Little Mermaid up enough for me to put her breasts back in their proper place. She had little pieces of gravel stuck to her back.

This beat the time that she threw up in her purse at some dive bar but got us thrown out; this beat the time I lost her at a bar and found her an hour later, passed out on the hood of my car, parked directly in front of the main door, as boys threw rocks at her; this beat the time she was dancing at another bar, got too close to the stage, and fell into the drum set, completely destroying it. And this certainly beat the time that she went to a party at her Danish then-boyfriend's parents' house and yelled to the other Danish guests, "*Shmorgedy borgedy norgedy!* This is America, people, so speak goddamned English!" When the boyfriend made an attempt to salvage whatever dignity either one of them had left, he picked her up and threw her over his shoulder like a bag of grain, only to hear the chilling gasps of seventy Danes as they witnessed the American girl peeing herself.

Tonight, however, she had earned her Ph.D. in the Stinkin'-Drunk Program. She had, without a doubt, exploded the night's Full Fun Potential limits, probably with the help of the Psychic Pregnancy lighter—and especially with the click of Joel's camera.

The Little Guy

When my best friend Jamie finally broke up with her evil boyfriend who had the personality of a raw potato, I considered it a hallowed day. It was the kind of relationship in which she had to carefully hide all of her best qualities, the qualities which I most admired in her: her pack-a-day devotion to Benson & Hedges, the talent she possessed to effortlessly paint a verbal masterpiece of profanity that could rival the mouth of any dockworker, and the facet of her that we called "Fun and Frolic Jamie," the portion of her personality that could be easily talked into anything after a twelve-pack. Like the night we found her drunk, topless, and unconscious in a neighbor's desert front yard, a photo of which may have contributed to the disintegration of the love between Jamie and Potato Boy.

I was thrilled when she broke it off, because this meant that I would be the sole beneficiary of half the pair of Page and Plant concert tickets Potato Boy had given Jamie for her birthday—in addition to a surprise weekend trip. At the beginning of that trip, their plane landed near a swamp. Jamie looked confused, though Potato Boy responded with an unmistakable glow and the smile of a retarded child in a toy store.

"We're in Salt Lake City!" he said gleefully. "We're spending the WHOLE DAY at the Mormon temple! Happy birthday!"

To an atheist like Jamie, it was a slight disappointment, especially since she had packed swimsuits and cabana wear instead of undergarments and shirts with collars. The trip then took a definite turn for complete horror when Potato Boy suggested that they really make it a special birthday and asked her to join him in a lifetime of happiness, fulfillment, and devotion.

She smiled and held out her hand.

It was the next logical step, he said, and she nodded with tears in her eyes.

Then he asked her to convert. He continued by saying that his entire ward had been praying for her soul to save her from hellish damnation, since it was apparent that she was gliding straight into the welcoming arms of Satan. When I heard that, I had no choice. I slipped the topless photo in the mail and licked the stamp.

After she told me the split was final, I jumped in my car and headed over to her house, making a pit stop at the drive-thru liquor store. When I walked through the front door, however, I saw her immersed in a full pout as she sat on the couch.

"I have all of the ingredients to make Fun and Frolic Jamie!" I said, waving a twelve-pack in front of her.

She didn't say anything.

"What's the matter?" I asked. "I bought imported!"

"It's not that," she said bitterly. "He kept the tickets! HE KEPT THE TICKETS!"

"The Page and Plant tickets?" I asked in disbelief. "Potato Boy kept the Page and Plant tickets? He doesn't even know who they are! He thinks they sang 'Jesus Is Just Alright.' "

"I know, I know!" Jamie said. "I just let him think they were a Christian band so he'd buy good seats. My dastardly plan has backfired!"

"Don't worry," I said quickly. "I know somebody who knows somebody who knows somebody who works for the concert promoter."

"It's a drug dealer, isn't it?" she questioned.

"You think it's a bad idea?" I asked.

"If he can get us good seats, I don't give a shit. I'll even throw in a copy of the topless photo," she said.

Two days later, I got a package from FedEx with two Page and Plant tickets in it.

I bestowed these upon Jamie, but there was still one more problem.

A long time ago, when we were in seventh grade, we went to our one and only dance ever. Jamie was haunted by a short boy who had, judging by his aroma, bathed in a boiling vat of Brut and smoked several cigars. He chased her all night, until he begged her so shamefully to dance when "Stairway to Heaven" was played that she considered it charity and said okay. He held her tight. She held her breath. He nestled his greasy little cigar head on her shoulder. She spotted his dandruff. Then he popped a boner. It was a very long song. Even to this day, when that song comes on the radio, she actually smells the stench of cigars and cheap aftershave, and feels something little rubbing up and down her leg. It's torment, pure and simple.

"What if they play 'Stairway to Heaven,' and I can't get away from it?" she asked when I showed her the tickets.

I told her not to worry about it. I said I was sure that Robert and Jimmy were probably pretty embarrassed by that song by now, and, unlike Don Henley and Glenn Frey, who abandoned all of their Eagles pride by releasing "The Boys of Summer" and "Smuggler's Blues," they'd rather drink gas than play it.

Anyway, we had other issues.

"Remember," I told her, "when we go to the show, dress like you once drove a Camaro."

But when we got there, I wasn't at all prepared. Did you know that they still make ankle boots with fringe on them, and that tube tops are still alive and thrashing in certain parts of the city? I didn't. I thought for sure that elastic had some sort of expiration date, or a tag inside the tube top that was stamped BEST IF USED BY 1978. We were the only women in the whole damn arena wearing bras.

"Somebody needs to tell these people that Stevie Nicks doesn't even wear gauze anymore unless she has an infected flesh wound," Jamie said.

We decided to find our seats, which were not very good: directly offstage, but fourteen rows up and next to the stairs. We could see down into the backstage part, where all the equipment and roadies were.

That's when we saw an odd little foreign man in green shorts and argyle socks trying to squeeze his way backstage and, after a couple of ill-fated efforts, he finally succeeded.

He met up with a backstage guy who whispered to him, they both nodded, and they started making gestures with their hands as if they were measuring something, like a block of ice or a well-packed kilo of cocaine. The odd little man pulled something out of his back pocket and handed it to the backstage guy, and he took it.

We couldn't believe our good fortune. We were witnessing what was possibly a celebrity drug deal, and we couldn't take our eyes off it. We were hypnotized.

Until the little guy looked up and saw us.

"CAUGHT!" Jamie cried as she looked straight ahead. "He saw us! He saw us! Don't look over!"

We stared straight ahead for five whole seconds before curiosity bored a hole in my self-restraint, and I HAD to look over. I got caught six more times, and the last time we were caught spying, the little guy was giving us the thumbs-up.

We, cordially, responded the greeting. Thumbs-up.

"I play bongos," he yelled up to us.

"That's nice," we yelled back.

"I play bongos for Led Zeppelin," he insisted.

"Sure you do," I screamed back. "And my dad's the singer. You can forget it, we're not going to have sex with you, little man."

Just then, the lights went down, the opening band took the stage, and the real fun began. Everyone in the arena was either piss drunk or crazy drunk, and due to our choice seats on the aisle next to the center stairs, we got to see a bunch of people fall down. As the night moved on, the harder they drank and the harder they fell. And some just plain stayed down.

Except for one man. He stumbled down the stairs, beer in hand and more, oh, so much more, in his belly, and looked for a place to call his own.

"Hey," he slurred, tapping the man seated behind us, "move over. Move over there. Lemme sit down. I wanna sit here."

The man behind us stoutly refused, and the beggar continued down the aisle until he tapped another man a couple of rows ahead of us. I saw the man stand up, turn around, cock his elbow, and pop the beggar square in the jaw with a crack so loud I heard it over the band. It was so hard that the beggar man caught air as he was lifted off the ground and flew three rows back, spraying himself and everybody else with what was left in his beer, which I knew in my heart was pure backwash.

People clapped.

The beggar man didn't get the hint. He stood up, and, like the complete jackass he was, tried to shake hands with the man that had just busted his lip open. He probably thought that the punch was a manly way of kissing.

"Hey, clown," the other man warned. "You come near me and I'll clock you again!"

"WHY?" the beggar man whined. "WHY? You're the one who spilled my beer! Is that fair, man? My BEER!"

He was about to get another kiss, this one puckered up to his nose, when security galloped down and took him away as he kicked and screamed and bucked.

That was when I noticed that Jimmy Page looked odd. He looked like my Pop Pop dressed up in my Nana's clothes, but his face was wide, as wide as my butt. I was staring at his face when I saw another face jumping up behind him, smiling widely and happily.

Thumbs-up!

"Jesus, Jamie!" I shouted. "The drug dealer's onstage! The drug dealer is onstage, and he's got a bongo drum in his hand!"

"I know," she answered with a laugh, "but your dad's having a little trouble with the high notes."

And there he was, our odd little man, dancing, playing, and waving at everyone, singing along. Our little guy. We were proud. We were really proud, especially when he had his little solo bongo-drum part, when the camera captured that smiling little face and projected him across the three big screens above the stage. That was our guy!

He was having a great time, such a great time that after everybody left the stage, he remained, as if the thousands of people were clapping just for him.

Well, at least we were. We were clapping for him and for Page and Plant, who had the very good sense not make us climb the Stairway to Heaven.

The odd little man stayed, long after the rest of the stage had fallen dark, with the thunder of the crowd still roaring, looking out at them and smiling broadly, with his thumbs raised straight up toward the sky.

I doubt that Potato Boy, down in the good seats, had as much fun.

Run from the Border

I saw the big brown sign first as we came over the hill and descended into the valley below. I slumped down in the passenger seat of the Trooper, hoping that my friend Jeff either hadn't seen it or had had his fill.

I just shook my head. It was like a bad dream. Ever since we had left Roswell, New Mexico, and headed back to Phoenix on our annual summer road trip, I had been tortured. I was at Jeff's mercy for survival since I had blown all my money, but I couldn't help it. How could I say no to the round of T-shirts depicting the sad aliens killed in the 1947 crash, which I had bought for my family at the UFO Museum in Roswell?

And there was no way that I could pass up a visit to the Ten Million Dollar Museum and Quick Mart, which boasted having a ten-thousand-year-old Cliff-Dwelling Baby mummy on display, even though admission was fifteen bucks. Jeff, who adamantly declared that his vacation wasn't going to include viewing corpses, stayed outside on a wooden bench and smoked.

When I found the Cliff-Dwelling Baby inside a case that

butchers traditionally use to display fresh steaks, it had a huge head and yellow skin, and was all curled up in a ball. It looked like it stank, and was lying in a basket with a bunch of straw and a mean Cliff-Dwelling-Baby look on its face that told me it was mad about being in the Ten Million Dollar Museum. Right next to it was a mummified Cliff-Dwelling Fetus, which resembled the aliens on my T-shirt, only much smaller.

Before I went outside to meet Jeff, I made a mistake by buying a Lunchables at the Quick Mart to eat in the car. As soon as I opened it, I started and could not stop thinking that the Lunchables meat probably smelled a lot like the Cliff-Dwelling Baby, and that if I ate it, it would be a lot like eating Cliff-Dwelling-Baby flesh, and I made myself sick.

So as a result of my squandering, I was forced to do the only thing I could; as I climbed into the Trooper, I handed Jeff the last twenty-dollar bill left in my wallet and said simply, "Take care of me."

It was then that I sealed my fate.

Jeff had taken quite a fancy to a new, super-hot Wild Jungle Burrito that Taco Bell had placed on its menu for a limited time only, and was determined to eat as many of them as he could before the time expired. This included stopping at every Taco Bell he spied between Roswell and Phoenix, and because I was now his charge, I had no choice but to oblige. By the time we hit Tucson, I had eaten more Taco Bell food than God had ever intended for one human being, and I was afraid that once I got home, my digestive system would no longer be capable of handling anything solid.

As we pulled into the parking lot that I prayed Jeff hadn't

seen, I knew I couldn't do it anymore. I just couldn't. For the last two days, I had consumed nothing but little cups of Pintos 'n Cheese and Cinnamon Crispas. Jeff had eaten his body weight in Wild Jungle Burritos, sometimes ordering five or six at a time and nibbling the leftovers as we drove through lonely stretches of desert road.

He pulled to a stop right in front of the double swinging Taco Bell doors and hopped out. I stayed planted firmly where I was.

"C'mon," he said as he motioned. "I'm hungry!"

"No," I said simply. "I'm not getting out. It's too much. I can't take it anymore."

"So you're going to go hungry," he said sarcastically.

"I guess," I pouted. "I can't eat any more beans. And you shouldn't either. The inside of this car smells like three days of death."

"I have to eat here," Jeff insisted. "I don't know when they're going to stop selling Wild Jungle Burritos. It could be at any time!"

"Then will you please give me three dollars so I can get chicken nuggets," I said, pointing across the street. "There's a KFC right there!"

"A bean-and-cheese burrito is only sixty-nine cents," Jeff pushed. "You could buy three and a half burritos for that much."

"Please, Jeff," I pleaded, "please can I eat Kentucky Fried Chicken? I'll just get a biscuit or some coleslaw. I need to chew something!"

"Then get a taco," he insisted. "Maybe you should have thought about this before you spent all of your money."

"Then just give me fifty cents for a biscuit," I cried. "I only need a biscuit!"

"I'll bet you wish you still had the fifteen dollars you spent to look at that dead baby!" he shouted.

I shook my head. "It was a mummy! The Cliff-Dwelling Baby was a mummy and worth every dime!"

"Your mother is never going to wear that dead-alien T-shirt!" he yelled. "You could buy a whole bucket of chicken for what you paid for it!"

I ignored him.

"You have a choice here," Jeff said sternly. "Either you march in there and order a burrito, or you're going to eat the Lunchables that's still floating around in the cooler!"

Honestly, what choice did I have? Eat beans or the Cliff-Dwelling Baby. Beans or the Cliff-Dwelling Baby. Beans.

I shuffled to the counter and got another round of Pintos 'n Cheese, and Jeff placed his order for five more Wild Jungle Burritos.

"I'm sorry, sir," the Taco Girl said. "We don't have those anymore. The limited time expired at midnight."

"I told you they were special!" Jeff hissed at me as I walked away with my little cup of beans on the tray, and I chuckled heartily as I raised the first spoonful to my mouth.

The Night
They Drove
Ole Laurie Down

Okay. This is what happened:

It was my friend Patti Pierson's birthday. We were all at our favorite bar to celebrate it with him on a Thursday night.

It was what you would call a slow drinking night. I only had four bucks to my name, which equaled one solitary drink as lonely as my soul. I ordered it and put it down before the clock even reached ten, sat on a bar stool, and then felt very sorry for myself.

I decided to try several approaches to score myself some more hooch. I'm a woman, I remembered. I have feminine wiles, and, besides, I've seen it done in movies. Look how successful Faye Dunaway was in *Barfly*, she had booze available at every turn because she knew how to utilize her estrogen, and she even looked like she smelled bad. I have a chance, I convinced myself, today I used deodorant, and I also vaguely recalled brushing my teeth.

I needed to practice first, of course, so I tried to catwalk. I stood up and swayed into the bathroom, thinking, Right foot first, swing out left hip. Left foot, swing out left hip, no, right hip, no, left hip. Oh Christ, I thought, this isn't going to work. I looked like a starving mule pulling a cart, or worse, a senior citizen missing both hips.

Damnit! I told myself, I know I can be sexy, if I can just let the sexiness out. Concentrate. Let it out, let the sexiness flow out of you, think of Gregg Allman, think of the sideburns, yes! Here it comes, here comes the sexiness, long blond hair, those beautiful shit-brown eyes, seduce, Laurie, seduce, open the floodgates of sexiness, hear it rush, oh yes, my arms are out-stretched and I am Whorie Laurie.

I slinked out of the bathroom like Sharon Stone in Gertrude Stein's body, real lustylike, and spotted my victim.

It was to be my friend John.

I leaned on the bar, lowered my head and looked up, batted my eyelashes a couple of times, smiled, as in "I WANT YOU BABY," and winked, flying in for the kill.

"You look weird," he said, and turned back to his beer.

DO NOT GIVE UP, the coquette in my mind screamed. KEEP BEING SEXY! WE'RE TALKING WHISKEY HERE! PRETEND HE HAS SIDEBURNS! "TIED TO THE WHIPPIN' POST!"

I blew in his ear, so delicately, like a little, almost unnotice-able breeze.

He put his beer down, turned, and looked at me.

"Are you all right?" he asked. "Did you forget to take your medication today?"

"I'm being carnal," I informed him in a whisper.

"You must be drunk," John declared. "You're trying to be a girl. I'm not going to buy you a drink. Get a job."

I shoved my dry ass back on the bar stool. The alcohol I had consumed wasn't enough to get an embryo drunk, and unless I started turning tricks behind the bar, I was going to remain broke, sober, and thirsty.

Patti, on the other hand, who was two beers away from residing in an alcohol-induced coma, announced to the bar via the PA system that all one hundred fifty people in the bar were welcome at his house for his birthday party after the bar closed.

His roommate Chris, however, missed the announcement, since he was cornered by a woman who had snakes wiggling out of her head, a woman that I recognized as his ex-girlfriend, Medusa.

I watched them. Her hands flew about viciously, several times coming dangerously close to his face, and her lips beat together as quickly as the hands of a clapping monkey. He wasn't saying a word. He stood there, dazed and mildly confused, waiting for the chance to escape. Chris glanced over at me with anxiety written all over his face, and I shrugged my shoulders. There wasn't much I could do.

She finally took a breath, and he beat it to the bathroom, which I thought was a smooth move. But when he peeked his head out from behind the door, there she was again, animated, angry, and yelling.

He walked out of the bar with her following inches from his heels as she barked at the back of his head.

It was last call, and I had sorely missed the boat. I accepted the fact that I was not going to get another drink, Whorie Laurie or not.

The bar was emptying out, directions to Patti's house were

being screamed through the gray smoke of the bar, and I headed for my car across the street.

As I pulled out of the parking lot and stopped at the traffic light, I glanced to my left, and there was Chris again, shaking his head as Medusa screamed at him.

I rolled down the window. I could hear her now, her voice screeching like a rape whistle, flames shooting out of her mouth.

I did the only thing that I could.

"Hey, Chris," I shouted. "You need a ride?"

"Hell, yes," he said and ran across the street and jumped into the passenger seat.

Undaunted, Medusa charged into the street, where we were held captive by a red light. She marched right up to my side and boldly stuck her head into the open window, flooding the car with bellows and thunder.

Chris calmly reached past me, hit the button on my door, and the window began to climb. She was still shrieking like a vampire caught underneath the sun as the glass grew higher and higher, higher and higher, until the pane stopped at the skin of her throat, and her head was stuck.

It didn't bother her; it didn't even daunt her. She kept roaring through the threat of decapitation, she could not move, and Chris desperately wanted to finish the job. I fought him for the button as the window zipped up and down, up and down, until I finally managed to smack the palm of my hand against her forehead, dislodging her skull from my car window.

The light had turned green. Medusa was still attached to us with one of her head snakes writhing above me, still caught in the window. I pushed the button again to release the serpent, and she took that opportunity to rear back into the car like a furious grizzly, her jowls dripping with rabid saliva and her eyes the color of burning coals.

Christ Almighty, she's going to eat us, I thought as I punched the gas pedal and tore through the yellow light as she took one last final swing and body-slammed my car.

We hadn't traveled farther than fifty feet when circus lights began to blink in my rearview mirror.

"Oh, no," was all Chris could say.

I pulled into the Mobil station at the nearest intersection and stopped the car. Officer Barney Fife strolled over and stuck his head into the window, which was still dripping and smeared with Medusa's sputter.

"Do you know why I pulled you over?" he questioned.

I shook my head.

"You had that girl's head stuck in the window," he informed me.

"I know," I answered. "She wanted to eat us."

"You were holding up traffic," he added.

"She was going to eat us alive," I stressed.

"Have you been drinking, Miss?" Barney asked.

Oh my God.

"Yes, I have. One drink. I only had four dollars, and I am a failure at being a whore," I replied.

"Step out of the car, please."

Shit, I thought, it's never good when they ask you to step out of the car, I've seen this on COPS. Bad Laurie, bad Laurie, whatcha gonna do, whatcha gonna do when they come for you?

"I'm going to give you a Field Sobriety Test," he told me. "Have you had any head injuries?"

Oh God, I thought, scratching my scalp. What constitutes a head injury? I fell out of the car drunk one night and hit my head on a river rock in the yard once, no, twice; I cracked my head on the toilet another time while I was passing out; I crashed into a telephone pole in the third grade on a field trip because I wasn't paying attention to where I was walking; my mom whacked me with a hairbrush on my eleventh birthday because I bit my sister.

"I don't think so," I decided.

"All right. This is what you need to do," he said. "Pretend there's a straight line here, and I need you to, heel to toe, start out with your left foot first, place it directly in front of your right foot, heel to toe, in back of your left foot, directly along the straight, imaginary line, traveling westbound, heel to toe, nine times, not eight, not ten, swivel with the heel of your left foot, spin a cartwheel, a back flip, heel to toe, complete a Flying Dutchman, and then do a back bend. Leave your cigarette in the car, please."

I had already practiced catwalking in the bar, so I figured that I might be able to do the drunk walk, although it seemed a little more complicated. And, if I do this, I wanted to ask him, do I get an endorsement from Wheaties? However, I recognized that this was no time to be a comedian.

I handed Chris my cigarette and began my routine, though I would have preferred to have background music, like Molly Hatchet's "Flirtin' with Disaster" or anything by Foghat. I began, heel to toe, heading westbound, nine times, outdid myself with a one-handed cartwheel, and flawlessly executed the back flip, although my aerial was a bit sloppy.

"Sorry," I said when I was done, "I have a slipped disc in my back."

Barney didn't believe me, I could tell.

By this time, two other patrolmen had stopped by to join the fun of administering a drunk test to a sober girl, the lights of their cars flying about, transforming the Mobil station into a full-fledged carnival.

"She's drunk," I saw them agree as Barney and his security guards with real guns, Goober and Gomer, nodded their heads in unison. "That girl smells like a still."

I had failed the coordination test. I failed it. And I was sober as the day I was goddamned born. They decided to proceed onward to the technical "pen and light" test, for which none of them was certified but they gave to me anyway.

It was at this point that I noticed all of the cars migrating to Patti's house, all the occupants of which recognized me in the Mobil parking lot, which by now had enough cops in it bugging me to qualify as a homicide scene. Some of the people I knew in those cars even waved at me after they honked.

Goober came forth with a Bic pen and flashlight in hand, and told me to follow the pen with my eyes without moving my head. He started off slowly, moving the pen to his right, my left, then moving it back, and all of a sudden the pen started whizzing around, darting back and forth, up and down, sideways, like the lights of a crazed UFO. I thought Goober was having a seizure, so I just plain stopped trying to play his game and looked him dead in the eye.

"I AM NOT DRUNK," I said sternly. If I was, the drunk test would have seemed like a lot more fun than it really was.

Goober, Gomer, and Barney huddled together, rock, paper, scissors, and in the third round they decided that maybe I was telling the truth.

"I'm going to give you a warning," Barney declared. "Don't hold up traffic anymore. You know, that third car behind you completely missed the light."

"That sucks," I said sympathetically.

"And don't do any more drinking!" he added.

"I can't," I replied. "I've run out of money, charm, and, apparently, luck."

I looked at Chris. He looked like he had lost a gallon of blood.

I lit another cigarette as we pulled out of the gas station and joined the caravan of cars headed to Patti's place. I realized then that I was lucky that I had absolutely no sex appeal whatsoever; if I had, I, without a doubt, would have been drunk, cuffed, and on my way to a new life and new job in the prison laundry.

Well, it might not have been so bad; maybe I could have found myself a nice girl and finally settled down.

This Is a
Public Service
Announcement

I hate public bathrooms.

I love and respect the sanctity of my own home potty; it may be as dirty as a truck stop, but at least I know the filth is mine, and I am free to do as I please or need. The fear of having to use a public bathroom is so horrible that I will do just about anything to avoid it.

When I was in sixth grade, my mother made me sign up for Girl Scout camp, and when I got there, I knew I was in for a long haul. The only way the facilities remotely qualified for the term *rest room* was because there was a light switch and a swinging bare bulb; other than that luxury, it was an outhouse, a long stream of port-o-potties lined in a row that smelled like the 4-H exhibit at the state fair on a hot day. The acoustics were incredible, and nearly echoed. What choice did I have? I held it for nearly two weeks and probably should have been hospitalized when I got home, but the pain that shot through my body when my intestines finally seized was nothing compared to the shame of pushing out a plopper within earshot of fifty Girl Scouts.

Even as an adult, I've noticed that some people don't play by the rules and terrorize other people in the potty. I have therefore documented several bathroom terrorists that have tormented me and countless other potty hostages, forcing us to hold it for unnatural periods of time. If you see yourself in any of the descriptions below, seek help. Cease your awful behavior before I am forced to do it for you.

Because I will.

The Trespasser: This violator is no friendly neighbor. She seeks pleasure by invading audio and aroma space of an already occupied unit by ignoring the "One-Stall Cushion" rule. She blatantly chooses the one next to it, despite groups of other available units within the vicinity. This action will automatically cease the operations being conducted in the already occupied stall, causing health risks and alarm. From a personal perspective, I can tell you that I try to use my turn-on/shut-off valve as little as possible so I don't wear it out and become incontinent by my next birthday, because they don't have transplants for those, you know. Try this catchphrase to remind you: "Beware of Fart, Stay One Apart."

The Hoverer: Perhaps to avoid using a time-consuming potty protector, perhaps to mark her territory, this offender won't let her bottom touch the seat, although it's perfectly OK if her byproducts do. Now, the target area of a bowl is rather generous, so the reasons for a misfire are rather mysterious to me, unless the participant is completely standing up and aiming from a corner. Hovering is never, NEVER acceptable behavior unless you just dug a hole in the forest. Remember this the next time you're tempted to resist a complete landing: "Don't Leave Your Mark, Just Sit Down and Park."

The Talker: Easily identifiable as the office chatterbox, the powers of this malefactor increase in strength once you are trapped in the same room and you're half naked. Starting off with something as innocuous as "How are you?" the Talker persists in conversation until your gastrointestinal system has recoiled and everyone else in the bathroom has discovered that your mom is a lesbian, your husband has left you, and there's a wart on your left hand. Words of caution: SILENCIO! Once the door closes on that stall, I am a nameless entity. If I am at work, I do not exist as Laurie your coworker, Laurie in the car pool, or the Girl That Everyone Hates. I am simply the Anonymous Pee-er. Do not attempt to make conversation with me. Do not ask me questions, and especially do not say, "BOY! Indian food again, huh?" When considering opening your mouth, let this come to mind: "Hear Me Unzip, Button Your Lip!"

The Waiter: Pity the Waiter. Unlike the others on this list, the Waiter is no criminal, sadly just a victim. Typically, the Waiter has urgent emergencies at hand, yet is too polite and thoughtful to shoot off a missile while others are present. The Waiter is often in pain, clutching her abdomen in order to keep her organs from exploding. She is minutes away from death. Unfortunately, many don't recognize the symptoms of a Waiter and hang around the bathroom like it was a free-sample booth at Costco. If you suspect there is a Waiter in your presence, leave immediately. If you are a Waiter yourself and sense that you are engaged in something of a Mexican standoff with another Waiter, call a truce, count to three, courtesy flush for background noise, then release. Offer to exit first, but only with the promise that the rival Waiter will not emerge until you have cleared the premises, lest you see each other's face. Don't forget now: "Silence, No Doubt; Just Get the Hell Out."

The Primper: If the Waiter has a mortal enemy, it is the Primper. I hate the Primper. HATE THE PRIMPER! If there's a horrifying sound a Waiter never wants to hear, it's the THUMP of a purse on the counter. Then the digging sound of the Primper's claws trying to find makeup, hairbrushes, and perfume. You see, I feel that if you cannot complete your prep work by the time you leave your house in the morning, you have completely forfeited your right to do so at any other point in the day. Your opportunity is over and you have lost your chance. Once, I was stuck in a bathroom waiting for a Primper to leave while my intestines threatened to shoot out of my belly button for hours. By the time the ordeal was over, it was dark outside, and everyone in my office thought I had gone home. So the next time you plop that feed bag next to the sink, recall: "Face of a Gnome? Do Your Makeup at Home!"

So all of you Trespassers, Hoverers, Talkers, and Primpers, beware. I'm waiting for you, ready to pounce from inside my favorite stall. And just because I haven't seen your face, it doesn't mean a thing.

I know your shoes.

Going Courtin'

It was 6:17 in the morning. I did not deserve this.

I don't even think the sun gets up that early, but there I was, listening to the radio as the alarm went off, fumbling through four empty cigarette packs before I hit gold. I had seven little soldiers left. Not enough.

It was going to be a long day.

The night before, I hadn't fallen into bed until four, and two hours' worth of tossing and turning certainly wasn't going to be enough to soften the blue bags under my eyes. What the hell, I thought, who do I have to impress? The court reporter? The bailiff? The judge?

I passed on dolling myself up, even left off the eyeliner. I searched the floor of my bedroom for my best Janis Joplin outfit (my groovy vest, my pants with the ripped-out butt, and my boots held together with electrical tape), shook off the majority of the cat hair, and got dressed. I slopped on the Secret and smoked a second soldier while I fed the Farm and started for the glory of morning traffic.

I was off to jury duty.

The summons had arrived at my parents' house several weeks before, and my mother was thrilled. She waved the envelope at me as excitedly as her smile was wide. I knew why. Nothing, not a package from QVC, not her new Miracle Mop that has a handle so she doesn't have to wring out the sponge with her hands, gets her as worked up as the possibility of one of her daughters encountering a balding, sexually repressed twenty-seven-year-old attorney strangled in a Perry Ellis necktie. She doesn't understand that the only way I would get close enough to a creature like that is if I were the defendant.

"Look what came today!" she exclaimed. "It's a job, Laurie, a job! You'll make twelve dollars! It's a very rewarding experience! And think, maybe, if you brush your hair, you'll meet a nice young lawyer, and then you can get married to someone who has a job like your sister is going to!"

I snatched the envelope out of her hand.

"Make sure you pack a lunch," she continued. "That cafeteria has horrible food. The ham is fatty. It was disgusting. I have never eaten a four-dollar sandwich like that in my life. I'll tell you, they have no business charging that price for food I wouldn't feed to my dogs or your father. The tuna looked good, but who the hell knows what they put in it? Remember, I was on a jury once."

Oh, I remembered. She spent two weeks convinced that she was a character out of a Susan Lucci Monday night movie who was involved in the most judicially important case in the history of the United States. Every night at dinner she would sit down and say, "Don't ask me about the Case. Don't ask me. I've taken an oath in front of God. Pass me the ashtray. I can't smoke in that goddamned courthouse, and I just have too many facts to think about in the Case."

My sisters and I deduced that the Case was probably something really cool like the trial of a transvestite multiple-personality serial killer or a kiddie-porn ring involving clowns that entertain at children's birthday parties, but it wasn't. It didn't even involve one single death. The Case was just all about some guy who hit an old lady in a crosswalk, bounced her off the car a couple of feet in the air, flattened her two-wheeled grocery cart, and then broke her hip. We were all very disappointed.

But not as disappointed as I was when I found out that I had to be at the jury assembly room at 8:30 A.M., coinciding with my deepest REM sleep patterns, which is usually when I dream of winning the cigarette lottery, that all of my pubic hair has just fallen out so that I never have to shave again, or that Gregg Allman asks me to be his old lady, we get drunk, and he tells me that Cher had more body hair than a silverback.

There I was, though, stuck in traffic and assaulted by a Journey rock block, smoking the third soldier and thinking that this was why I couldn't hold on to a real job.

I found the courthouse without any problems, probably because I've been there many, many times before for reasons I won't go into now. As I approached the steps, a woman jumped out of a station wagon and ran toward me, a brown bag in her hands. This is pretty brazen, I thought. Someone is going to try and sell me drugs in front of superior court. "Miss! Miss!" she cried, waving at me as she ran. "Are you hungry?"

Why, yes, I thought, I am, and nodded my head. I had run

out of Pop-Tarts the day before, fed the dogs the last remaining three slices of bread that morning, and attempted to drink the last of the milk until I discovered that it had become Brie overnight. Sure, I was hungry.

"Well, here," she said, shoving the bag toward me. "Here's something to eat, it's a sandwich and an apple."

Wow, I said to myself, my mother didn't tell me about this. I don't need the cafeteria, obviously my mother didn't know about the Juror Free-Lunch Program. She couldn't have complained about fatty ham then.

"Thank you," I said as I took the bag. "This is really cool."

She smiled and nodded. "Anything we can do to help. Where did you sleep last night?"

What a curious question, I thought. Who are you, the Morality Police? *Where did I sleep last night?* Sure, give me a sandwich and expect me to spout off my entire sexual history so you can get your kicks.

"Probably in a bed," I answered a little snottily.

"You don't remember?" she asked in a softer voice, tilting her head in a subtle action of pity. "It *was* in a bed? Was it at the women's shelter?"

What the hell? Then it hit me.

"OH MY GOD, YOU THINK I'M HOMELESS!" I said, throwing the bag back at her. "I am not homeless, I just didn't take a shower today, that's all. I didn't want to deal with eyeliner, OK? I am not homeless. I'm just dirty. *I am just dirty.* My parents live in Scottsdale, I swear. My mother gets her nails done. She was once on a jury, here, in this very building, really she was. I'm not homeless, for Christ's sake. I'm wearing deodorant."

And then I ran as fast as my lungs would let me up the stairs and into the building, into the juror's assembly room. I sat down, took a deep breath, and figured maybe I was reading too much Bukowski, and it was beginning to show.

Then I looked around. The assembly room looked like a trade show for Metamucil or Polident. I was the only person in the room that wasn't alive when a Roosevelt was in office. Boy, this was going to be a fun day, well worth the twelve dollars I was going to make.

I had to fill out a biographical form and watch a video hosted by Channel 13's Linda Hurley, who informed me that if I am dismissed as a juror, I mustn't take it personally, because, I was told, somewhere, in some courtroom, I am the perfect juror.

That's right, I thought to myself, my friend Junior is coming up for trial for allegedly selling acid to an undercover cop at a Sonic Youth concert, assaulting a police officer, and then resisting arrest. I'd be the perfect juror for that. And then I wondered if Junior was going to put all of his teeth in when he went to trial, to try to impress his jury. I thought that would probably be a good idea, especially because I've seen him without his teeth, which he considers optional, since he has to take his partial out when he eats. It's not very pretty.

After I thought about Junior, I sat there. And sat there. And sat there. I sat there while everybody else got called to a courtroom and got a juror's badge. I sat there while the woman next to me, Dottie, babbled incessantly about how she was a nanny and how she was a widow and how those kids just fill up her life now that her son is married to a public-relations person and just doesn't call her anymore. Dottie was happy that she got called for jury duty, because she felt good for being able to serve her country as a citizen, it was an honor and that she didn't see any better way that she could help her fellow citizens than to get drug dealers off the street. She looked at me and shook her head. I prayed for Junior.

At 3:47 P.M., while I was completely immersed in a show about lesbians who stole men's wives on *Jenny Jones*, my name was called just as a woman from the audience asked if all three of the involved parties had ever had sex together.

Damn! I thought as I stood up (before the lesbians could answer—damn!) and took my place with the other forty potential jurors, and I found myself standing smack next to Dottie.

Half of us filed into the elevator, standing shoulder to shoulder. Dottie's blue polyester rubbed against my cat hair, and I noticed that she smelled an awful lot like the ointment aisle at Target, topped by *eau de* Mother-of-God-you-really-need-to-sink-those-choppers-of-yours-into-a-fizzling-bath-of-Efferdent. As more people crowded into the elevator, her odor became more and more apparent until I thought I was going to be sick. When the doors started to close, however, Dottie shrieked and held up her hand.

"Oh no, oh no, oh no," she chanted. "I can't do this, I can't be this close to people! I can't! I'm losing my breath! This is too much! There's too many of you in here! I'm claustrophobic! I can't breathe! Oh no, oh no! I'm going to be sick!"

This is not happening, I told myself, this is not real. This old stinky-denture woman is not going to throw up on me. What did she have to complain about, I thought, she's the one that smells like a rest home.

"You must be a lot of fun on road trips," I mumbled to her.

With the imminent threat of all twenty of us, especially me, being doused with a firehose spray of vomit, the crowd in the elevator split in two, and with help from my not-so-gentle hand, Dottie was shoved to the front. She then placed her head up against the wall and took deep breaths in between trying to jump off the elevator every time it stopped, forcing the bailiff to drag her back in.

Unbelievably, we made it to the courtroom without bearing witness to the terrifying apparition of any type of bodily fluids. We took our seats, and I got stuck in the jury box. I could tell right away that the prosecutor hated me; I looked far too, well, homeless. The public defender, however, looked at me and just smiled a smile that said, "Oh, yeah, you look like the kind of girl whose man has done time. Let me see your tattoos. I've got Bart Simpson on my back. You're my kinda juror, sister woman."

Then the bailiff stood up. Her job was similar to that of Paul Shaffer's—a sidekick or straight guy of sorts—and introduced the judge. Dottie burst forth with a hearty round of applause. The judge strutted in, sat down, and then started asking us questions, just like David Letterman. It was like a talk show, but we didn't have any lesbians on that I knew of. Did I have a problem with prosecutors? Had any of them treated me unfairly? Was a member of my family a police officer, sheriff, deputy, or security guard at K mart? Had I ever been on a jury before? Did my husband work for the county attorney's office? Boring, boring, boring.

Then from out of nowhere, the judge belted out, "This case

concerns a DUI. Do you know anyone that has a drinking problem?"

I don't know anyone that *doesn't* have a drinking problem.

"Do you know anyone that has been involved in Alcoholics Anonymous or an addiction recovery program?"

That's how I met my second-to-last boyfriend.

"Do you know anyone that has been involved in a DUI?"

Uh-oh.

The college-aged, clean-cut law student in the back row raised his hand.

"I was involved with a DUI several years ago, but the charges were reduced, and I did community service."

What a nice boy, the rest of the jurors thought, community service. Now that's respectable, he's paid for his sin by mowing church lawns. He's all right with us.

The slightly older, thirtyish-looking man in the button-down, pressed, and starched white oxford raised his hand.

"I was involved with a DUI approximately ten years ago, but I'd rather discuss that in private."

A little suspicious, the jury considered to themselves, but he's obviously ashamed of what he's done, since he doesn't want to talk about it. It was probably all a mistake, anyway, he looks so upstanding. He's probably a good person.

The girl in the front row raised her hand. She's wearing all black, her pants are ripped, her hair isn't brushed, and she smells like cigarettes. She looks like a bag lady.

"Um, I was pulled over for a DUI three weeks ago, I failed the Field Sobriety test, but they let me go anyway. Oh, and I wasn't drunk."

All seventy-eight eyes of the jury turn to the girl in black, the DRUNK GIRL, she's the reason society is crumbling, she's the epitome of our decaying morals, we want to know where she slept last night. Sure, she wasn't drunk. Wonder what she had to do to get out of that DUI. We know. WE know it all, DRUNK GIRL. And you think you can come in here and be on a jury with us regular folk? Think again, Whore of Babylon. Go back to the bar.

Dottie nodded her head as she looked at me. She knew she was right about that girl the minute she'd laid eyes on her. She wished she could sentence me, what better thing could she do to service her fellow citizens?

I didn't care, and when my name wasn't called during civic duty first cuts, I wasn't surprised. The public defender, however, looked at me with sadness in his eyes. He knew the Drunk Girl probably would have voted to have his client walk.

Who knows?

. All I know is what Linda Hurley told me; that I should not take it personally. Dottie didn't know shit, because somewhere, in some state, in some county, in some courtroom, I was the perfect juror.

Yep, I was the perfect juror.

Just as long as I dressed in an Ann Taylor suit, washed my hair, and lied straight through my unbrushed teeth.

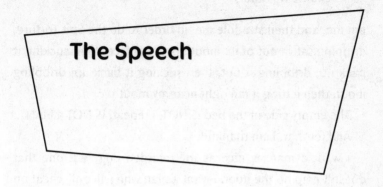

The Speech

Relationships suck.

They suck hard.

Sometimes, in the middle of the night, when my bedroom is as black as death, and the sheets on half the bed are as cold as a five-day-old corpse, I think

All I ever wanted to be was someone's Old Lady.

I want to be the ball and chain.

I need to be somebody's squeeze.

I float in this for a minute, in this bed that is too big for me, and feel a little bit lonely when all of a sudden the wheezing, flopping noise from my lungs wakes me up and shocks me back into Relationship Reality, and I realize

The empty side of the bed does not fart in its sleep.

The empty side of the bed does not attempt to sodomize me while I am sleeping.

The empty side of the bed does not make me look at the turd as big as my leg grounded in the toilet and then ask aloud, "Dude, do you think it will go down in one flush?"

The empty side of the bed does not wrestle me to the floor,

pin me, and then straddle me, in order to do the Spit Torture, dripping saliva out of its mouth over my face, then sucking it back up; dribbling it out, then sucking it back up; dribbling it out, then letting it fall right near my mouth.

The empty side of the bed IS NOT, I repeat, IS NOT a MAN.

And for that, I am thankful.

I want a man as nice as my retarded dog, but one that doesn't crap on the floor. I want a man who will only cheat on me a little and who will call me once a week. I want a man who will buy his own drinks and who will hold back my hair when I puke. I want a man who is unconfused regarding his sexual identity. I want a man who has never heard of or practiced the Speech.

I will never find him. He has never been born.

The last time I got my walking papers, it was over the phone. "It" had lasted about five months, the longest-standing Relationship Record I had held in this decade. Well, it wasn't even a "relationship." I called it the "thing." He didn't call it anything. He thought I wanted to get married tomorrow, have seventeen kids, buy an Isuzu Trooper, and then staple his scrotum to the living-room couch. All I really wanted was one phone call per solstice.

Anyway, the conversation was off to a running start when he cleared his throat and said,

"I am not ready and will not be ready to actively get involved with anyone for at least three to five years."

"Why?" I asked. "Are you going to prison?"

"No. What I am saying is that I'm not ready to commit to anything, either way."

"Either way? You mean you can or cannot commit to committing or not committing?" I said, growing suspicious and confused. "Are you giving me 'the Speech'?"

"I think we should concentrate more on the 'Friends' part of our—well, you know."

Suspicions confirmed. I gasped.

"You ARE giving me the Speech! You just gave me the Speech! That was the Speech!" I cried.

So I got the Speech, which automatically drops you to the lowest point in life, it's like throwing the self-esteem balloon on a cactus. You become such a small specimen of existence that you could probably mate with yourself, which would actually be such a terrific advantage.

I guess I took it well. I didn't set anything on fire, practice any voodoo, or listen to sad songs. No, this time I just sat at the bar and drank, sneering and growling at all of the men except my friend Dave.

"How's it going?" he asked.

"Well, I got the Speech today," I said.

"Oh no. Not the Speech," he said. "Did he use the 'F' word?"

I nodded.

"Oh God." Dave sighed. "The 'F' word is low. Low down."

"Yep," I said. "*Friends.* He said, 'We're just Friends.' "

I don't understand the Speech and how men learned about it. Was it a part of boys' eighth-grade PE class, did the gym teacher make them say it to one another over and over in the showers so they would be good at it?

"Okay, now how does it go?"

"It goes, 'You're a cool girl, and I like hanging out with

you, but I'm not ready to make a—um, that big word—commitment to one person, and I think we need to be . . . we need to be . . .' "

"Man, this is the most important part! The 'F' word, man! The 'F' word!"

"Oh, yeah! You tell the chick you want to be Friends! But you don't mean it, do you?"

"No. A chick won't let you nail her if she knows she's not even a Friend."

Or maybe the Speech is some kind of computer chip that gets implanted in every baby boy's dingle as soon as he's born.

"There are things running around out there with uteruses, son. You're going to need this."

Could it be a hormonal gift package with an added feature thing, where women get PMS with estrogen, and men get the Speech with testosterone? I don't understand it.

I do understand one thing. I am pissed off at God for making me heterosexual, and I swore that the next time I heard the Speech, I was going to fix that. I have enough Friends, so I'm going to try really hard this time to be a lesbian. The only problem with this is that all men are fascinated by lesbians, lesbians are delicacies to men, and once they find out you are one, they want you back again.

But maybe it's just my destiny to remain alone, eating single-people food like Soup for One, collecting Precious Moments figurines, and thinking that my dog can talk back to me. Oh, God. With any luck, I'll wind up living in a trailer park as a bitter, celibate alcoholic with a heart full of hate. I'd much rather be alone and make myself miserable than give someone else the pleasure. I'll die a graceful and glowing death when my cigarette plunges into the shag carpet as I pass out after my final date with Jack Daniel's, who will be resting very comfortably and very drained on the pillow of the empty side of the bed.

Moral Sex

My nana was getting aggravated.

I couldn't blame her. She was stuck in a hospital room with an inflamed gallbladder while her pain medication was lolling about on a nurse's cart somewhere in the hallway. To make matters worse, we were minutes away from watching President Bill Clinton's apology for diddling Monica Lewinsky, and the coverage clogged every channel.

"I don't understand all of the fuss," Nana said, shaking her head at the TV. "There wasn't this much news when Frank Sinatra died, and he was much more important to this country. He was a real American."

Sitting in a chair next to the bed was Nana's sister, Aunt Ida, an exact duplicate of Nana, right down to their four-foot-ten height, their wavy light-brown hair, and their tan Easy Spirit shoes, and she wasn't pleased about the lack of television viewing choices, either.

Personally, I was more concerned with keeping Nana's ID bracelet on her wrist, lest we discover three years from now that we brought the wrong Nana home from the hospital and then have to share custody with another family. The day before, just to be safe, I pulled a bobby pin from her hair and scratched the letters N-A-N-A into the polish of four fingernails on her right hand after she got a pain shot and passed out.

"The whole thing is crazy, I tell you," agreed Aunt Ida. "Who wants to see the president naked? Now I got all these pictures going through my head. I don't need that!"

If Monica Lewinsky had seen naked pictures of Bill Clinton beforehand, I can assure you that this whole thing never would have happened in the first place. I've only seen photos of him with his shirt off, and that was enough to make me do the cootie dance. Big nipples, size of silver dollars, on saggy man boobs, and they were purple. The color of eggplants.

"What kind of girl would keep a dress for such a long time with that . . . *stuff* on it?" Nana said, pointing to the TV. "That pig! She's never heard of a dry cleaner?"

I was amazed. My nana, the eighty-two-year-old embodiment of everything good and pure, who has never had a bad word to say about anyone, was getting testy. And, most horrifying of all, she knew what "stuff" was.

"Ah, she's a tramp," Aunt Ida said, waving her hand. "She's just one of those girls—Laurie, what do you call them, they follow men who do the rock and roll?—"

"Groupies," I offered.

"Groupies!" Aunt Ida finished. "They'll do anything."

"Oh, yeah. A grouper. Like Ava Gardner was to Frank Sinatra," Nana added, shaking her head and wringing her hands. "He got into so much trouble with her. So much trouble . . ."

"Don't play with your wristband, Nana," I said cautiously.

"What do they mean by 'inappropriate relationship'?" Nana asked as the president spoke across the airwaves.

"It means they were fooling around," Aunt Ida said. "But in different . . . ways."

"Like what?" Nana queried.

Oh, boy. Now you see what you've done, Monica Lewinsky, you stupid, stupid tart, I thought. Because of you, I have to explain to my nana, while she's in a hospital bed with an enlarged gallbladder, what oral sex is. Do you see the damage you've caused? Do you see where your sinful path has led?

Ever so reluctantly, I bent down and whispered into Nana's ear exactly how Lewinsky got to know President Clinton "in the biblical way," and when I was done, she looked up at me, bewildered.

"I don't know what the hell you just said," Nana whispered back. "You know that's my bad ear."

Forced to do the devil's work twice, I repeated the carnal carnage in the good ear.

She scrunched up her face. "Oh, that's disgusting," she replied, thinking it over in her mind. "I don't understand why they call it 'moral' sex. Was it approved by a priest?"

"No," I replied slowly. "Just by Monica's mother."

"This president," Aunt Ida said, "he wears his privates on his sleeve like they were cuff links."

"This is not a nice girl, Ida," Nana reminded her. "She's a floozy. Even President Kennedy didn't pick girls up off the street. What's this all over the inside of my hand?"

"It's your address and phone number," I said quickly. "We'll wash it off when you get home."

"I think I have the coordinating map on my arm," Aunt Ida mentioned.

"Oops," I said, embarrassed. "Sorry, I guess you got too close."

A nurse entered the room armed with a shot of Demerol and pulled the curtain around Nana's bed.

"Oh, this is really binding you," I heard the nurse say to Nana. "Let's take this off."

"No, no, no," I asserted to the curtain. "Leave the wristband on. Nice trick, but I've got her marked."

"You're a nurse," I heard Nana say from the other side of the curtain. "Do you know what 'moral' sex is? My granddaughter says it's dirty."

"Why do you have a piece of paper that says, 'I've Been Switched, And I Miss My REAL Family! Call Police!' taped to the back of your neck?" the nurse asked Nana.

"I thought I felt something itchy," Nana said.

After Nana got her shot and the curtain was pulled back, the nurse shot me a look and left the room. That's when I noticed a white pair of Nana's slacks folded at the foot of the bed.

"Is this what the nurse took off?" I asked Nana, and she nodded.

"Nana," I started, "you've had these on the whole time?"

"Yeah," she answered.

"But you've been here for three days," I said. "Why didn't you tell me?"

"Oh, I wanted them on," she answered. "I was worried that if I had to walk to the bathroom, someone might see my legs."

"Monica Lewinsky could learn a thing or two from you, Nana," I said.

"Oh, no," she replied, the Demerol kicking in. "I was married for three years before I had your mother. I have my paper from the priest. That's very moral, isn't it?"

I nodded and smiled. After she drifted off to sleep, I pulled another bobby pin from her hair and scratched the letters I L-O-V-E into the polish on the five fingers of her left hand.

Men Are Stupid and I Rock! (Ode to Dorothy Parker)

I was stood up last night.

Again.

I waited at the bar for, well, all night. I kept glancing at the door every time someone entered, pretty much every fifteen seconds. A couple of times I thought I saw him, a flash of hair, a slight smile, but on a double take it wasn't him at all, it was someone a couple of inches shorter, with crooked teeth. His teeth are straight. Perfectly straight and white, a Pepsodent smile that I would've liked to kick in with the heel of my boot.

The son of a bitch. I had eaten an entire roll of Clorets already, just in case he came in without me seeing him first. I could talk freely and easily without having to talk into my hand and then smell it, no, no dead animal breath here. I had cool, minty, kisssssssable breath.

I looked good, too, in my opinion. I had only two pimples, and my eyeliner went on smoothly, no tire tracks tonight. I had even used lip liner so that the lipstick smeared on my lips wouldn't bleed into the little crinkles above them. I wore perfume.

I sat on the bar stool for hours, holding in my stomach in a desperate attempt to appear alluring. At a quarter till one, I still hadn't given up and imagined him bursting into the bar, out of breath, panting. His car had broken down. He's run, not jogged or walked, he's run, five miles, nonstop, to get here. He looks around frantically, scanning every face in the bar, where is she, am I too late? He sees me, that ivory Pepsodent smile extends across his face, and he's every bit as handsome as I ever thought he was. I have waited. My patience has paid off. He holds my hand and I am not mad. Everything is fine.

Instead, the lights above started to flicker on and off; the bar was closing. I killed what was left of my drink, sucking out every last drop of whiskey with the tiny red straw until the ice crashed together. I walked out of the bar, just a little bit too sober, and headed for home.

It's the next morning, I wake up.

Immediately, I think:

He stood me up, goddamnit. I knew he would, I knew he would, I knew he would. God! Shit! How could I be so stupid! I knew he wouldn't show up, why did I wait? So stupid, so incredibly stupid! I am the jackass. It's me, I admit, who is the jackass. I'm raising my hand. IT'S ME. Christ. All night I waited, he said he'd be there and he wasn't, just like he should call me today and he won't. Oh no. Oh no. No, I won't do it, I won't, I will not sit here all day and wait for that phone to ring I WILL NOT DO IT. I absolutely refuse to sit and look at that dead phone, no, no, no, he got me once, he won't get me again I WILL BE STRONG. Damn that phone it better ring and it better ring right now. RIGHT NOW.

I take a breath. I look at the phone. It looks back at me. It blinks.

I will smoke. I will have a cigarette, and by the time I'm done, the phone will ring. I deserve that much, I do. I deserve an explanation, and when I hear it, no matter how much bullshit he spews over the phone, I will not be pissed off. I will pretend not to be pissed off. In the meantime, I will count how many drags I can get off of one cigarette. I have never counted before, I will be interested to know, to find out, just how many times I can inhale on this cigarette.

One drag.

Just one ring, one little jingle; it's not too much to ask.

Ring.

I will make it ring with my mind, I will make it ring, if I think hard enough, it has to happen.

Two drags.

I'm thinking, thinking hard, I can make this phone ring. Come on, please phone, ring.

The phone looks at me again, shakes its head. Nope.

Piece of shit. Three drags.

I promise I will not be mad if that phone will ring. I will be nice. Pleasant. Charming. "No, no, it's quite all right," that's what I'll say, "don't worry about last night. I understand, truly I do."

Four drags. Am I kidding? He stood me up! Who the hell does he think he is? Gregg Allman? Because if Gregg Allman stood me up, I could never be mad, hell no, he's Gregg Allman! Goddamnit. I will not let him make me feel this way. I am a woman. Women are strong, much stronger than men.

You know what? I don't even want him to call. I don't. Even if he calls, I won't pick up the phone. I'll just sit here and laugh is what I'll do. You're goddamn right. I'll laugh. Ha ha ha. Let it ring a million times, I'm not gonna pick it up. Asshole. The next time I see him, I'm gonna punch him. Square in the gut. And I'm going to walk right up to him and say, "I hate you." No, then he'll know that I'd waited. I'm not going to say anything at all. I'm not going to let him know that I waited. I won't give him the satisfaction. No! I'm going to tell him that I'm sorry that I didn't show up! Yes! I'm going to call him right now and tell him that.

Eight drags.

Where's the phone number? I should call Jamie, she would know what to do. She could tell me if I should call him or not. She would say don't call him. Don't call him. Here it is, here's the number, I hope I wake the bastard up, I do. I'm dialing, I'm dialing, I'm done dialing, it's ringing. Oh my God, it's ringing. What the hell am I doing? It's ringing. Shit. What if a girl answers? Hang up the phone now!

I slam the phone down and push it away, evil thing. I dig voraciously through my nightstand until I find a big, thick black marker, pull off the cap, and victoriously mark his name and phone number out of my telephone book and out of my life.

HA! Thought you got me, but you didn't. I am not going to call you, I will not be the fool in this circus, no way, little man, find yourself another idiot, buddy. I'm not going to play your games, count me out.

The cigarette is gone. I've lost count. I pound it out in the ashtray.

That's right, I am a woman, I come from a long line of women, my mother was a woman and so was my grandmother, yes, she was a woman, too! I like being alone, I can do whatever I want, I don't need him. What is he? Someone to make me feel miserable, to make me cry, a dog is what he is. All men are dogs. I LOVE ME. I love doing anything I want, whenever I want. I don't need anyone else to make me feel fulfilled or satisfied! I wish I could call myself! I wish I could date me, I am a wonderful person, and it's his fault if he can't see that!

Wait a minute—I don't remember hearing a dial tone when I picked up the phone, I don't think there was one. I know I'm late on the bill, I'm sure of that, but I don't remember a dial tone. Maybe the phone is shut off. He's probably been trying to call all morning and can't get through. Oh no. I feel horrible. The phone is shut off, I bet; that's why it—*stupid*. Moron. I didn't hear a dial tone, but I *did* hear it ring at his apartment. Idiot girl. Serves me right. I was getting all ready to forgive him, but not now. Hell no, not now. He can go to hell. Straight to hell. Dance with the devil, for all I care.

But what if something happened, a car accident, food poisoning, testicular cancer? What if he's dead? He's listed in the phone book, the white pages, I'll find it, F, F, F, G, Gr, Gra, Gri, yes, okay, it's right here, I'm dialing again, I hope he's not dead, don't let him be dead. It's ringing, it's ringing, it's ringing—

"Hello?"

He answered. HANG UP NOW! *Slam!*

You sonofabitch. You son of a bitch! You're alive! Damn you! Oh God, I can't believe this! I must be crazy, I must be out of my mind! How can you do this? You're alive and you didn't call? How dare you be alive and not call me! You are NOT Gregg All-man!

Light another cigarette. One drag. Two drags. Three drags.

I'm going to rip this page out of the phone book, is what I'm going to do, and then I'm going to set it on fire. I'm going to watch it burn. Here we go, it's going up in flames, it's being eaten by fire, now I can't call him if I wanted to, four drags, five drags, six drags. Never again. I will never fall for that again. I've learned my lesson. If I've learned something from this, then it was worth it. The lesson is, don't trust him. And don't trust men. Don't trust anybody. I'm the only one I can depend on. Today, I hate everyone from now on, everyone but me. I am independent. I am a lone wolfess.

The phone rings. Quietly at first, ringing almost in a whisper. The second ring is louder, more like a cry. The third ring begins to yell, and before the fourth ring even happens, the phone is shrieking and instead of ripping it out of the wall the way a good woman should, I pick up the receiver.

And it's guess who.

"Did you just call?" he asks.

"No," I answer, "I was sleeping."

"I'm sorry about last night," he says.

"It's okay," I lie. "I understand. Truly I do."

"I'm glad you're not mad," he sneaks.

"Want to go to the game tonight?" I mention quietly. "I have really good seats. The game's sold out."

"Yes! I do want to go," he says. He's excited now. Really excited.

"Good, meet me at the arena," I continue, "around eight o'clock. I'll wait for you there."

"See you then," he says, "at eight."

And he was on time, got there a little bit early, actually. He looked up every fifteen minutes, every time a girl with long brown hair passed him.

I know this because I saw him standing outside the main door, and as I watched him, I laughed. I laughed, sitting in Jamie's car parked across the street, deep in the shadows where he couldn't possibly see me.

Oh, yeah. It's called karma, baby.

Survival of the Fittest—Well, Kind Of

I had high hopes for the May morning after my college graduation. I cleared all the food and crumbs out of my bed the night before, tucked the blankets in securely, placed a pack of smokes, a lighter, and a Pepsi on my night table, and tacked two black sheets over the bedroom window so that the sun couldn't sneak in before I was ready to get up at three.

I forgot one thing.

It seemed, as soon as I got home, my head sank into my pillow, and my eyes rolled back in my head, something shrieked in my ear. And that demon from hell was the phone.

Impossible, I immediately thought, as my brain sourly attempted to flicker on, impossible, no one I know functions well enough at this point in the night to remember a phone number, let alone *dial* it. No one would dare to violate the sanctity of the Two O'Clock Rule, which used to be the Twelve O'Clock Rule until 75 percent of my friends decided to become unemployed and we voted to have the rule amended to two o'clock. The Two O'Clock Rule states, more or less in its entirety, that "it is against Holy Nocturnal Law to purposefully and intentionally disrupt and shatter the sleeping patterns of those who condemn and shun daylight, especially when those persons are inebriated, with a phone call or social visit. Doing so may kill those comatose with loud sound vibrations, as will the exertion of speaking." The only exception to this rule that we could think of for making a phone call before this appointed time concerned the efforts of a troubled friend trying to make bail.

There is no one I associate myself with that would execute a phone call so repulsive in its conception, no one I know that yearns to communicate with me while I am hung over and woken suddenly because when I am, I'm nastier than when I'm drunk. There is no enemy, no ex-boyfriend, no creditor, that will dare to experience that—especially before I have my first three cigarettes and go to the bathroom. There is no sane person in this world who would dare go there—no person except my mother.

Before I even screamed "WHAT?" into the receiver, I heard her say, "For Christ's sake, don't tell me you're still sleeping! I've been up for eight hours! Haven't you let the dogs out yet? It's no wonder they crap all over the floor, you keep them locked up so damned long."

"You're killing me, Mom."

"Did you find a job yet?"

"I'm almost dead, Mom," I said, wondering if my mother had swarmed on my sister, who had also graduated the day before. Then I suddenly remembered that, unlike myself, my sister possessed qualities of responsibility, ambition, and survival instincts, whereas my survival instincts consisted solely of lighting an entire pack of cigarettes end to end because I only had one match.

"Have you applied anywhere? How are you going to support yourself? Your sister already has three interviews."

"I'm hoping I can sell some crack to grade-school kids, and then if I still don't have enough money I'll turn a couple of tricks," I mumbled.

"Don't play funny with me. Your father and I aren't going to support you forever."

Okay, so I had been living on the dole while I was in college, collecting my allowance of seventy dollars a week from their house every Thursday, which is when I would also steal food, because seventy bucks does not stretch far. And every Thursday, my mother would hand over the three twenties and a ten all folded together tightly, and proclaim as it touched my fingertips, "And don't spend this at the bar buying drinks for all your friends."

My mother was convinced that I was living as glamorously as someone who had another of Mick Jagger's babies. "What do you do with all of that money?" she asked me one Thursday after she'd caught me stuffing my father's Oreos into my purse.

I ran down the list. "Twenty dollars for gas, seventeen for a carton of cigarettes, and twenty dollars for dog and cat food," I answered. "And that leaves me thirteen dollars to live on."

"Well, if you didn't spend all of that money on gas so you could drive to bars and on cigarettes, you might have enough money to buy your own food," she said.

"And then you'd find me with seventy dollars clutched in my hand, swinging round and round from the ceiling fan with a noose around my neck," I said earnestly.

I lived through this summer on the dole, trying to find a job after three o'clock during the days and trying to find drink specials at night that would stretch my thirteen dollars of mad money from Thursday to Thursday. Those were the salad days.

I didn't find a job until the end of the summer. When I told my mother I had an interview, I knew tears of elation were swelling down her cheeks, drowning her cigarette. "Thank God," she wept, "thank God. You have an interview for a full-time job. It is full time, isn't it?"

"Yes, Mom."

"We are so proud of you. Your sister has an interview, too. Actually, now she has five."

I went to the interview with my résumé in hand, and I even wore a dress and panty hose with the crotch still intact. I sat on the couch in the reception area and was euphoric to find an ashtray on the front desk full of smashed butts. This is a great and holy place, I thought. People smoke here. My kind of people.

My new potential boss walked through the door, and a familiar face was he, though I couldn't place him right away. We started the interview, and I noticed he was looking at me strangely—like he knew me, too. I looked back, and then it hit me, though not all at once:

Fourth of July, earlier that year; I am very drunk. I am going to my friend Kate's house for a barbecue, I slam the front door open, exclaiming, "I want to set something on fire!" and throw all fifteen pounds of my purse down next to a long-haired man sitting cross-legged on the floor. It lands with a solid THUD, and he starts rummaging through it and exclaims, "Look at all this shit! You've got a fifth of Jack Daniel's in here!" and begins

to throw away what he thinks to be insignificant empty cigarette packs, little scraps of paper, and gum wrappers. I am immediately offended and frightened that he may want some of
the bottle, so I scream, "Who the hell are you, little man?" kicking him as hard as I could in the leg.

And that little man is the same little man sitting across from
me now.

He looks at me quizzically. "Do you know Kate?" he asks.

"I DON'T KNOW ANY KATE," I blurt out.

"Didn't I clean out your purse, and you—"

Oh, shit. This is the part of your life, Laurie, when your
past comes back to haunt you, remember? Your mother told
you this would happen. You always thought it would take the
form of kinky photographs, but you never wanted to be Miss
America anyway. You'll never get off the dole and seventy-
dollar Thursdays. Never, never, never. You'll never get a job
where you can smoke at your desk, you loser. Just confess.

"YES I WAS THE ONE WHO KICKED YOU AND CALLED YOU
'LITTLE MAN.' BUT I WAS DRUNK. IT WAS A HOLIDAY. IT REALLY
WAS."

And I got the job.

I am a receptionist.

I work every day.

I make the coffee for the Little Man.

I make more, though not much more, than seventy dollars a
week.

My sister also got a job and came over to tell me the news.
She makes seventy dollars in a day.

"I got the job!" she cried.

"So did I!" I cried back.

"I have my own office!" she said.

"I have a swivel chair!" I said back.

"I have my own phone extension!" she exclaimed.

"I learned how to put toner in the copier!" I exclaimed back.

"I have my own business cards!" she shouted.

I smiled. She may have had the cards, she may have had the voice mail, but there was no way she had the prime perk that I did.

"Who gives a rat's ass?" I shouted back, about to embrace victory. "I can smoke at my desk!"

And that's what I call survival instinct.

Extreme Clean Sports

The box in my nana's carport was bigger than she is and twice as wide.

"I just want to bring it inside," she said, throwing her hands up as my sister, her husband, and I stared at the box. "You never know, with all the rotten kids running around here who might come by and steal it. And then what would I do?"

"I don't know," I said. "I have no idea what's in this box, although by the consonants, Q, V, and C printed all over it, I sense that my mother has some connection to it."

"Yeah," Nana nodded. "She said the doctor said I needed it, but I don't remember hearing that."

Several weeks before, my mother and Nana ended up in the emergency room after they had attended a baby shower, at which Nana broke her arm.

"I don't know what happened," my mother later recounted when they returned from the hospital. "We were heading for the platter with the little chimichangas on it, and the next thing I know, Nana dropped like the *Lusitania*. Never even made a sound, God bless her."

"I didn't want to be any trouble," Nana offered. "I thought if I was quiet, no one would notice."

"Of course not," my mother agreed. "Who's going to notice an eighty-two-year-old woman with a broken arm laying on their living room floor in between the enchiladas and the spinach dip? Yeah, Ma, you looked just like a rug."

The doctors then conducted a battery of tests on Nana to try to find out why she fell down in the first place, although none of the professionals seemed to think that her three-inch high heels might have been a contributing factor.

One of the doctors then examined Nana's bones and asked her if she exercised. I really don't know what he expected her to say—"Oh yes, I'm a lightweight contender on the kickboxing circuit," or "I can bench-press more than your IQ"—but after a careful ponder, she looked at the doctor and told him, "Well, at the mall, I walk a lot in between stores. It's a long way from Easy Spirit Shoes to Sears."

"That doesn't count," he apparently answered, and told her to begin a routine on a regular basis. "You have to be more active."

I guess that doing a load of laundry, making your bed, pulling weeds in 114-degree weather, vacuuming the entire house six times, and pounding chicken breasts into paper-thin cutlets every day isn't considered a "regular, active routine." My nana keeps a house cleaner than a Gap store and has the endurance of a short, compact athlete. You could easily perform a triple bypass on her kitchen counter using her pizza cutter and salad tongs without the slightest risk of infection. In my book, that's more than active, that's called "extreme clean sports."

I mean, come on. The woman is eighty-two. When I'm eighty-two, all I plan on doing is sitting in a chair, spitting on people, and gumming bits of chocolate until they're soft enough to swallow whole. Push a vacuum cleaner? I'd spit at you.

In any case, what my mother heard the doctor say was that Nana needed to get in shape, and since Nana doesn't drive, the gym needed to come to her. And it sure did.

In the shape of an enormous brown box.

"I still don't understand," I said as we looked at the box in the carport. "What is it?"

"Oh, it's one of those *things*," Nana tried to explain. "I don't know. I get on it, put my feet into slings, and walk without touching the ground like the astronauts."

"I don't like the sound of that," I answered honestly, and my sister agreed.

"I have a feeling it's the same E-Z Glider you bought me after I had my insides ripped out as I was giving birth to your son," she said, pointing at her husband, who just shrugged. "It was almost as good as the diamond ring I was expecting. I got on it once, fell off it once, used it to hang sweaters on and then sold it at our garage sale for seven dollars. It was a great drying rack for bras, though."

My brother-in-law hauled the box inside, cut it open, and started putting the pieces together. Along with the skeleton of the E-Z Glider was an instructional videotape that Nana popped into the VCR.

In the video, a squat, buff little man with the tiny arms of a T. Rex was pumping away on the E-Z Glider, spouting off on how easy it was to operate.

"Just get on and go!" he proclaimed as his legs swung back and forth, and his petite squirrel arms pulled the handles in opposite directions. "Let's get to know one another! Tell me something about yourself! Tell me why you want to enhance your life with the E-Z Glider!"

Dear God, I thought as chills ran up and down my spine. Why do I have a feeling that the E-Z Glider will be listed next to "Cause of Death" on a coroner's report with my nana's name on it? I could just see her hanging on for dear life as her legs swung wildly below her, her little Nana voice crying out to the video in between panicked breaths, "MY NAME IS CONNIE! I WALK AT THE MALL BUT THE DOCTOR SAID THAT WASN'T GOOD ENOUGH!! I CAN'T FIND THE OFF BUTTON! I CAN'T FIND THE OFF BUTTON!!!!"

On the TV, the video cut from the midget-arm man to a scene with a couple making love in the frothy waves of some beach, to keep Nana motivated, I suppose.

"That's disgusting," Nana said as she clucked her tongue and just stared at the screen. "This is filthy. I hope this isn't part of the exercise."

"Okay, Nana," my brother-in-law said, tightening the last bolt. "It's all ready."

"I really don't think this is a good idea," I protested. "Nana, I'll take you to the mall every day. We can walk from Easy Spirit Shoes to JCPenney and then to Sears! I just don't feel good about you using this thing!"

"Oh, I'm going to use it, all right," Nana said, looking it over. "I think I can fit three whole bras on here!"

Amy's Mom, the Fairy, and the Hedge Clippers

I usually never answer the front door when someone rings the bell. Never.

I made it a force of habit after countless bored, middle-aged men kept coming up to the door inquiring about the aging, disintegrating 1968 Oldsmobile rotting in my carport under a thermal blanket of dust. I would explain that the car didn't belong to me. They'd offer me money. I would explain that it belonged to my father. They would ask why he didn't wash it. I would explain that the whole thing was a restoration project he was going to start when he retired. They would tell me that's why they wanted it, too. I would then explain how my father entrusted to me the car's only existing set of keys in case I needed to move it during a fire. They would ask me if the car still ran good. I would explain that I had no idea. I had placed the keys in an old jar for safekeeping, but by mistake had not realized that some silica-gel crystals at the bottom of the jar would dissolve any kind of metal in a matter of three years, which was how long it took me to open the jar and discover that the keys had turned into little metal matchsticks and that I was scared shitless to tell this to my father. Only then would the men go away.

I got tired of telling the story, so I quit answering the door.

One Saturday, something changed. I don't know what, but the doorbell rang, and before I could stop myself, I was turning the knob and opening the door.

Through the screen door I saw two short figures, one of whom was wrapped in an explosion of pink tulle and sequins. As I stared closer and tried to understand what creature was before me, the other one spoke.

"Hi," it said.

"Hi," I replied hesitantly, slowly recognizing them.

"We're from down the street," it continued.

"I know," I said, finally realizing what was on my front porch. They were children. Girl children. One was dressed up like a ballerina. And they were each carrying a pair of hedge clippers.

I shook my head. No one is going to believe me, I thought.

"Can we cut your bushes?" the bigger one asked. "We like cutting bushes, and we've been in business for two years."

"You've been cutting bushes since you were two?" I asked.

"I'm *eight*," she sighed disgustedly.

"And I'm six," the ballerina said.

"Does your dad know that you have those?" I asked, pointing to the clippers that were as tall as the ballerina's shoulders. "They're kind of dangerous."

"Oh, yeah, he knows," the older one said. "He told us to do it."

"Well, I'm sorry, but my bushes were just cut," I lied. "But if they start getting crazy and growing out of control, I'll run right down to your house to get you, Child Bush Cutters."

"Okay," the big one said, rather disappointed as she started to turn away.

"Out of curiosity, how much would you charge me?" I asked, not knowing that, essentially, I had a big stick in my hand and was getting ready to poke a big, mean bear with it.

"However much money you had in your purse," the ballerina offered.

"What if," I replied, "I only had a nickel?"

"A nickel would be fine," the big one said. "We're supposed to get six hundred dollars from Amy's mom next week."

I was confused. "Are you Amy?" I asked the ballerina.

She replied that she was Staci, and the bigger one was Casey.

"Amy's . . . kind of our sister," Casey said.

"Why is Amy's mom going to give you six hundred dollars?" I probed. "Is that how much money she had in her purse when you cut her bushes?"

"No. It's because we have custody of Amy," Casey informed me.

"Oh," I said, deciding not to say anything else.

"Vicki and her live-in boyfriend attacked my mom," Staci, the six-year-old ballerina, said.

"Yeah, and Vicki drives up and down the street trying to figure out where we live," Casey added.

I was confused again. "Who's Vicki?" I asked.

"*Amy's mom*," the girls said together.

"How did Vicki attack your mom if she doesn't know where you live?" I asked.

"She didn't attack her at home," Casey told me. "Vicki attacked her at the courthouse. She punched my mom in the neck."

"We were glad that Amy's mom went to jail," Staci added. "But it was only for one night."

I didn't want to know anything else about Amy, her mom, or the courthouse; I had heard enough to know that it wasn't any of my damn business.

"Can we pet your dog?" Casey asked, peering in the house.

"Sure," I figured, letting them in. "Keep the hedge clippers on the porch, though."

"Cute house," Staci said as her pink tulle swept inside and she looked around.

"Thanks," was all I could manage to say.

A half-hour later, the girls were sitting on my couch, eating Pop-Tarts and drinking iced tea. They had filled me in on every other detail of their lives, including the facts that Casey had four dads, while Staci only had three; they had to take their dog for a walk later that day because the Realtor was coming over, and if she saw it, they would all be thrown out on their butts on the sidewalk; they were vegetarians, and did I think that maybe I could give their mom and dad some sugar because they hadn't had any in a while for their coffee. I was sitting at the kitchen counter, also drinking iced tea, and wondering how the hell to get them out of my house.

"I have to start fixing dinner soon," I announced.

"For us?" they said together happily.

"No," I said. "I don't think you'd like what we're having."

"What are you having?" Casey asked.

"Um, just a lot of meat," I lied. "Big pieces of meat."

"Do you have a husband?" Staci asked.

Although I knew that she understood the concept of a "live-in" boyfriend, I lied again. "Yes, I do," I stuttered. "And he's a big meat eater, but I think it's time for you girls to go home now. I'm sure your mom's worried."

"I bet she's not," Casey said.

"Bye," Staci said as she petted the dog. "See you tomorrow!"

"Um, I work tomorrow," I mentioned quickly.

"We'll wait till you get home," Casey said. Staci nodded.

I felt bad. I felt bad that they didn't want to go home, that no one gave a shit where they were, and I felt worse when I realized that they were more than likely smarter than their parents. I felt bad as they walked out the door and down the driveway with their huge hedge clippers in both hands, but I knew better than to think that Staci and Casey were my problem to solve.

I kept thinking about them up until my live-in boyfriend came home, and when he walked through the door, I made him sit down right away.

"I've got to tell you this before I forget one detail," I insisted.

"Wait," he said, waving his hands. "I have to tell you this first."

"But you won't believe what happened this afternoon," I stressed.

"You won't believe what I just saw," he interrupted.

"Mine's funnier," I insisted.

"Impossible," he replied.

"You wish," I shot back.

"I just saw those two little girls from down the street cutting our neighbor's bushes with hedge clippers, and one of them was dressed up like a fairy!" he exclaimed.

We laughed, and it all seemed pretty funny until he called me at work the next day. He was home and he sounded kind of angry.

"Your fairy friends are here, and they won't go away," he said, almost in a whisper.

Apparently, he had been relaxing after work when the doorbell rang. He, having better sense than I, did not answer it. So the girls rang the bell more, and more, and more, and eventually just left a finger on it until the bell did nothing but ring.

"They finally stopped ringing the bell," he continued, "and that's when I heard them crunching around the gravel in the front yard. They're looking for you, they're peeking in the windows, and I'm in my underwear! I had to close the doors to all the bedrooms, and I've been trapped in the hallway for the last thirty minutes!"

I thought I heard, from his end, the sounds of little children screaming something at the top of their lungs. "Are they singing?" I asked him.

"That's not singing," my boyfriend confirmed, "those are sounds of demons being freed from hell."

Then he held up the phone so I could hear the evil chorus of the bush-cutting fairies shrieking, "LAAAAAAY-DEEEEEEE! LAAAAAAY-DEEEEEE! LAAAAAAY-DEEEEEEE!" over and over again, trying to seduce me out into the front yard.

"I'm sorry," I offered when he came back on. "I won't answer the door anymore."

"No, *lady*, you won't," he snipped. "As soon as they go away, I'm putting on some pants, and I'm welding it shut!"

It's okay, I thought to myself, I hardly ever use that door, anyway.

Make Me Laugh, Clown

I'm afraid of clowns, I'm not ashamed of it.

Mrs. Lee, my third-grade teacher, once invited one particularly angry clown, Frosty, to perform at a classroom holiday party. This was the same teacher who had developed her own brand of discipline by placing a dog kennel, previously used by her then deceased Great Dane, next to her desk and locking children in it when they misbehaved.

Upon Frosty's arrival, he bore a distinctive scent, one that as an adult I can now identify as gin, and when Sherry Pierce, the perfect third-grade girl who had hair she could sit on, mentioned this, he just looked at her and chuckled. The clown began his Clown Fun, which entailed knocking the kids on the head with a plastic squeaky hammer, pulling a mottled piece of red foam out from behind their ears, and creating balloon animals in obscene shapes. The clown got even testier when Michael Moorehouse, the obligatory chunky child, told the clown he wasn't funny. Frosty immediately lunged into action, swiping Michael's snack plate and saying, "I'll show you funny, fatty," and took a bite out of the green-frosted cupcake and reindeer cookie.

The clown trauma didn't end there. It simply matured when I was at a friend's birthday party the next year and witnessed the hired clown entertainment relieving himself in the backyard by a wooden fence while the cake was being cut. That was when I really began to understand about clowns, and that I should try to avoid them. That they were insidious creatures, agents of the devil. My aunt used to have two clown paintings in her living room, and this sealed my belief. Both paintings of the sad clowns boasted thick, bloodstained-red smiles hiding fanged, splintered, yellow, pointy teeth, and the single teardrop. I was convinced that as I passed those paintings, they would call to me, "Laurie, we're your friends. Put your hand in front of our faces. We'll show you what funny is."

As an adult, I feel capable of defending myself against a mime with a jolt from a pretend stun gun or a very real sucker punch, and then running away very fast. Clowns, however, are a different story. They carry forces of the dark side with them, impenetrable by any act of retaliation. Pop a clown's balloon, and he'll only mutilate a bigger, nastier one. Lock him in the trunk of a car and he'll multiply himself into six more clowns. Spit on a clown and he'll only want to give you a hug. I hate clowns so much that I become immobile and hypnotized with fear as soon as I see one. I think all clowns should go to clown prison for all of the very real damage they've done to America's youth. They already like wearing stripes, so that's not a problem, and instead of ostrich meat, Sheriff Joe could just toss a pack of balloons and some cans of Silly String into the cell and say, "Here you go, creepy clowns. Make your own damn lunch!"

I'd rather take on a band of collection agents armed with copies of my credit history than mess with a clown. I'm convinced that there's a Clown Underground Network, and if you mess with one, you're messing with the whole hive. Word gets out. You're flagged, and if you're within a five-mile radius of a rainbow fright wig, it will seek you out and trail you relentlessly, trying to give you an imaginary flower. If you take it, you've succumbed to the Dark Clown Power. Before you know it, you'll find yourself trying to stuff seventeen of your friends into a Volkswagen Jetta that you've just slapped a multicolored CLOWN PRIDE bumper sticker on.

I don't understand what kind of person would want to be a clown, I really don't. I don't understand what's hiding behind the red-rimmed eyes, the pasty white makeup. Maybe it's better that I *don't* know, that the secret isn't revealed. I have a suspicion it's not fit for human eyes. Some people pay up to five hundred dollars to go to clown camp for a week to take such classes as "Beginning Balloons," "Advanced Balloons" (I'm sure Frosty took that one), and "Strategies to Scar Children So They Become Frightened, Emotionally Crippled Adults." The literature for this camp states that it prepares its students for when someone walks up to them and says, "Make me laugh, Clown." It goes on to say that "great clowns are not made in a week but a lifetime," and the camp will help people "complete their clown selves." There's also a picture of an anorexic man in a shiny, black, scoop-necked unitard demonstrating a clown dance, and another one of "Bojo showing students how to walk into doors." Most people I know don't need to shell out five hundred dollars for clown college to learn that. They just need a couple of beers on an empty stomach.

I don't know about you, but I've never once been tempted to call on a striped demon to make me laugh. That's like asking someone with periodontic disease to use your toothbrush. You're just inviting danger. When I was a student at Arizona State University, I passed a clown standing on the mall and deliberately did not make eye contact. That persistent clown followed me from one end of the university to the other, showering me with balloon poodles and stick men, and trying to squirt me with battery acid from the flower on his lapel.

On the steps of the communications building, I finally turned around and assumed battle stance, my knees bent, my fists pulled. "No, clown!" I yelled. "No means NO!" The clown started to pretend cry, but I shook my finger at him. "You stay away from me!" I warned. That's when I believe my name and likeness were distributed throughout the network, because two days later, while I was visiting my grandparents, my Pop Pop gave me a gift.

It was a clown doll with evil yellow eyes and a pointy hat, dressed in a polka-dot jumpsuit. The Network had gotten to my grandparents.

"Get it away from me," I said, shielding myself with my hands. "You're dabbling in clown stuff you don't understand!"

"Put it outside, Nick," my nana said to Pop Pop. "You know what happens when you make her nervous. I don't want to clean up any mess."

"NO!" I said, jumping up. "NEVER let a clown out of your sight! It always has to stay in your field of vision! Don't turn your back to it!"

"She's so cute, though," Pop Pop said.

"She won't be that cute when she comes alive at night and stuffs your windpipe full of confetti," I warned. "Besides, how do you know it's a she?"

"Oh," Pop Pop said as he smiled, "because I named it Laurie."

How I Can Relive the Horror of High School for $103

I remember that it was a hot June night; the lights on the football field were searing and white, making it seem a hundred degrees hotter than it really was. You could see the silhouettes of the moths and the bugs zipping around in bright circles, as well as the floating dust in the air as a result of a couple thousand people walking around. I was sitting on a metal folding chair, one of 547 that had been set up in the gravel in front of the field.

I was seventeen and an hour away from starting My Life. It was the early eighties; I was wearing white pumps. I was fanning myself with the ceremony program, trying to keep my face from melting into my lap. Someone called my name, I walked across the stage, grabbed my high school diploma without falling down (I didn't drink then), and went back to fanning myself until the ceremony was over.

I walked off the field a high school graduate, met my mother and father in the swarm of Killer Parents that had descended on the field afterward, and lit up a cigarette in front of the principal who had tried to suspend me for smoking on school grounds a couple months before.

I had forgotten about that night for a long time. There was no reason to think about it, anyway. I had forgotten all about it until I got a letter in the mail with the return address listed as "First Class Reunions."

Sweet Jesus, I thought when I found it in the mailbox that I hadn't checked in a month, I'm going back to high school.

Well, I've changed a bit since I was in high school. Back then, I said no to using and selling drugs, I washed on a regular basis, and I still had good credit. Since then, my inner thighs have grown together, my lungs have filled with enough tar to pave the highways of the continental United States, I cannot have a phone installed without my father cosigning for it, and I have entirely forgotten what sex is like with another person and am convinced that I'd have to use WD-40 on my private parts should the opportunity present itself.

There was only one place that I could read this letter, and that was on the toilet, with a lit cigarette in my hand.

I opened it. "It's time for your high school reunion!" the letter shrieked, and then went on to inform me that 546 of the people that I hated most in the world were coming together at some lah-de-dah resort for the entire weekend to talk about the good old days. It was going to cost me sixty dollars to sit across from someone like Jim Kroener (who bounced a basketball off my head when I was a junior), eat a bad Cornish hen dinner, and try to make polite adult conversation on Saturday. Then there was the option of the "no-host mixer" on Friday, which meant that I would have to fork out a small fortune to be able to control myself and not lunge at Jim Kroener's eyes with a bottle opener in my hands. For the Grand Reunion Finale, the reunion committee had scheduled a Family Picnic on Sunday to "show off the kids." I could also purchase a commemorative T-shirt for ten bucks, a photo memory album (for which I could send in a recent photo of myself) for thirteen bucks, and a Bio-Data book, whatever the hell that is, for another ten.

The grand total for the sentimental bonanza screeched in at $103, not including the Saturday 8:00 A.M. $57 golf tournament hosted by the school's only "celebrity," someone who played a season of football for U of A. The real celebrities of our graduating class are still serving fifteen to twenty in Florence State Penitentiary for an incompetent bank robbery in which the getaway car was a '74 powder-blue Pinto.

The dinner was out; no way was I going to consider spending a Saturday night with a thousand Mr. and Ms. Livin' Larges, flashing diamond rings, pictures of the offspring, and breast implants. No Thank You. The picnic was also out. I have no children (thank God for genetic sterility), but I could bring my rabid dogs in the hopes that they would attack Jim Kroener's kids.

I decided that my only possible appearance would be at the no-host mixer, where instead of paying for drinks, I could just suck off the bottle in my purse.

Attached to the letter was the Bio-Data form that asked all of the vital inconsequential questions (name, occupation, marital status, children, tax bracket. Answers; Laurie, none, none, none, I don't know, let me ask my dad). I briefly considered scrawling DECEASED over it in black marker, until I saw the part that asked for "Your Fondest High School Memory." I jotted down the memory of when my best friend, Jamie, and I had to dissect a cat in biology class so we skinned it, made it into a marionette with the use of string and tongue depressors, took it for a walk down the hallway, and made it wave at people until one girl who saw it threw up in a big trash can. The Bio-Data form also asked for "Your Message to Your Classmates," so I wrote an eloquent little paragraph that included the phrases "three-headed children," "foreclosure," "prostate cancer," and "yuppie bastards."

Also listed was the high school trivia contest, consisting of the questions "Who was the senior-class president?," "Who was homecoming queen and king?," and "Who was the valedictorian?," the answers to which I had no idea, but I still know the names of all the girls in my class who had VD or got pregnant.

Finally, the letter advised me to "call the baby-sitter, go on that diet, make those hair and nail appointments, and mail in your registration form today!"

Well, my dogs don't need a baby-sitter, like hell if I'm starving myself for a bunch of balding, overweight insurance salesmen and dental hygienists, and I'd pretty much have to see the Four Horsemen of the Apocalypse smoking crack in my driveway before I stepped one foot inside a beauty salon to get my nails done.

Instead, what I plan on doing is getting Stinkin' Drunk, bailing my man out of jail, and heading off to the ten-dollar no-host mixer. And maybe, if I'm lucky, I'll find and scrape up a dead cat on the way there so the entire class can remember the good old days just like I did.

In Bell-Bottoms and Boots, You *Can* Go Home Again

"I'm not going in. I'm not. No way."

Jeff stopped the car in the dead center of the parking lot and looked me square in the face. His face was white, his eyes were little balls of ice, and he was serious. "I am *not* going in," he said.

"Shut up and park the car," I replied. "We're here now. I said park the damn car."

"Did you see those banners?" he asked, motioning to the pirate's flag that waved so precariously in front of us, belching, WELCOME BACK!!! "Did you see what was in there? Blondes in prom dresses! One of them had chopsticks in her hair! I thought I saw a lawyer! We'll probably have to flash them a platinum American Express Card before we can even get through the door!"

Jeff was nervous. I could tell by the way he was pounding his fist into the steering wheel and by the way torrents of tears were plunging down his pallid cheeks. Yeah, he was nervous, if only because he graduated from the same high school that I did, though one year earlier. He knew exactly what was lying in wait, ready to ambush us as soon as we crossed into the wicked, unforgiving terrain of nostalgia. And he was only my date, as well as the only person who reluctantly agreed to travel through this seventh gate of hell with me to my high school reunion.

I was nervous. My hands were shaking as badly as they do after a night with a fifth, and this was compounded by the fact that I had never sent in the registration form or the fee required to attend the reunion. In essence, we were crashing. And like *hell* if we weren't going. It was the first time in ten years that my face was clear, and I had brushed my teeth real careful so that my gums wouldn't bleed.

"Jeff," I said as delicately as my personality would allow me, "I have waited years for this, years to show these people what I've become and who I am, like that song that Gifford woman sings on those boat commercials."

"You mean 'If My Friends Could See Me Now'? Is that the song you mean?" he quipped. "The song about your high school friends being jealous because you're a receptionist and a drunk, and you get thrown out of bars nightly because you don't agree that one o'clock is a good time to quit drinking? The song about all of your high school friends being jealous because you scare the hell out of every man you date with your foul mouth and violent physical outbursts, guaranteeing yourself a lonelier existence than both the Brontë sisters combined? Is that the song you mean?"

I hated Jeff right then because he had a point. In the years since I had graduated, my finest accomplishment had consisted of collecting enough Marlboro Miles to send away for a three-bedroom double-wide Marlboro mobile home, complete with floor-to-ceiling gold-veined mirrors in the master bedroom. There wasn't exactly a whole lot of stuff in my life that I could brag about without sounding like a passage from the autobiography of Squeaky Fromme.

"So, Laurie, what have you been up to since high school?"

"Well, the DEA ransacked my house in 1986, all of my credit cards were taken away in 1988, and last year my boyfriend left me because he got a teenage red-headed hippie girl pregnant."

And this was my life.

"Okay, Jeff," I said. "I'll pay for your drinks all night."

"Why, look, here's a parking space."

We waltzed through the parking lot, past all of the leased Acuras and Lexuses, the sole of one of my cowboy boots fixed to the upper part with the aid of black electrical tape. We approached the banner and the name-tag table.

It was constipated with the aging, squealing officers of student council, and I quickly pushed Jeff ahead of me while they exchanged business cards. I grabbed a name tag off the table, peeled it, and slapped it over my left breast. I was now Jens Hansen, and I had crashed my high school reunion.

"Are you sure we're at the right place?" Jeff whispered. "It looks like a Hair Club for Men convention."

"Yes, we're at the right place!" I hissed. "I think that's Susan Woods trying to hoist her four-hundred-pound butt out of that innocent plastic chair."

We decided that we needed a drink before we talked to anyone, so I sent Jeff to the bar to get himself a beer and to get me some mixer, ice, and a stirrer.

Before I could even mix my drink in the bushes, I heard, "Ha-ha-ha! *Laurie Notaro?* Is she still alive?" and I saw one of my best high school friends talking to our favorite teacher, who'd divorced his wife and three kids to marry the eighteen-year-old cheerleading captain a year after I graduated. Before I could get the dirt on him and his child bride, I bumped into another good friend of mine who was chatting with my high school enemy.

"Guess what!" my friend Joanne screamed when I saw her. "I gave birth! It was like shitting out a pumpkin, and I don't recommend it!"

Joanne had gotten married, had a son, lived within two miles of my house, and liked being a housewife because she could smoke all day and watch TV. My rival had also gotten married, moved to Ventura, gotten divorced, hated her job as a special-ed high school teacher, and had to borrow a cotton floral number to wear to the occasion. Her life was still "really great, though." She also had some girlie freak-out idea that she and I were soul sisters during high school. The only reason I might have liked her then was because she had a butt bigger than mine, and, standing next to her, I was a dish.

"Oh, I love palazzo pants!" she cried, motioning to my outfit. "I love all the new styles!"

"These aren't palazzo pants," I said, lighting a cigarette. "They're 1972 black-polyester, silver-thread bell-bottoms. Ninety-nine cents. Family Thrift Store."

She tried to recoup. "Well, look how big your purse is. You must be a mom too!"

"Hell, no!" I answered, flashing the neck of the Jack Daniel's flask. "I just have a drinking problem."

I mingled. I laughed loudly. I smoked a pack, with Jeff at my side. I realized that the more that people insisted that they loved their lives, the more they really hated them. I realized that I was the only one of our graduating class that still got carded for cigarettes. I realized that I was one of only three unclaimed women that had never gotten married, divorced, annulled, impregnated, Lamazed, dilated, or employed as a high school teacher. As the three of us stood together—myself, Kathy, and Laura—I figured that if we were overweight, had any types of careers or even decent jobs, and were of any ethnic origin whatsoever, we'd probably have our own sitcom on Fox Television called *We Have a Better Chance of Being Shot by a Terrorist Than We Do of Catching Ourselves a Man or Six Breasts for Hire.*

As the night came to a close, I promised to stay in touch with Joanne and fumbled through my purse for a hidden pen. Frustrated, I dumped out the contents on a round table: cigarette packs, gum wrappers, unpaid bills, razors, the flask, and the pen. As I wrote down Joanne's number, the president of the senior class, who had a fabulous and absolutely fulfilled life as a divorced high school teacher, turned from her audience and snickered, pointing to the razor. "You carry a *razor* with you?" she said in her typically condescending tone, one that hadn't changed since we all had spiral perms.

"Well," I replied, "you never know when you're going to need to shave in a hurry."

"And what's *that*?" she asked, pointing to the bottle and gawking.

"Oh, this?" I said, picking it up and putting it back in its proper place. "I figure that this is a little more fun and a lot less expensive than getting involved in a failed marriage and then spending ninety percent of my time fighting about who gets the sectional sofa in the settlement."

I then stood next to the homecoming queen for an entire fifteen minutes without even knowing it, because she had bought herself a brand-new face. I thought she was a LaToya Jackson female impersonator until Joanne told me different. Even though, at that moment, a flashback popped into my mind of her jumping onto a table in the cafeteria one day and belting out her own rendition of "Fame" to the freshmen and sophomores who were trying to eat their lunches, I felt such pity that I couldn't even vomit on her.

As I walked back through the parking lot to Jeff's car, a little drunk and almost out of cigarettes, I laughed, and Jeff and I agreed that the reunion wasn't so bad. I didn't have to make up anything about myself, because as pathetic as I think the thing called my life is, it kicked ass over having to pay a baby-sitter when I got home on Sunday morning. Not only that, everybody was especially impressed when they discovered that I had my own personal stalker.

"You know, Jeff," I said, "That wasn't so bad."

"No," he said as he opened my car door, "it wasn't. In fact, if the homecoming queen was picking chunks of your dinner out of her hair at this very minute, it could have even been fun."

We drove out of the parking lot and headed for the nearest bar for the last twenty minutes of drinking time. I lit my last cigarette effortlessly, with calm, smooth hands. They had stopped shaking, they were completely still, and I hadn't even noticed.

Open Wide

I can almost handle going to the gynecologist because, supposedly, like every other female, I'm only supposed to go once a year.

Supposedly.

Well, as luck *and* my cervix would have it, I got to see a whole lot of my gynecologist this year, though she got to see a whole lot more of me.

In any case, I know better than to expect that anything connected with me would ever go smoothly or be considered routine. If things didn't happen that way, it would make me *normal*. The life of a freak, on the other hand, is filled with snags, bitter disappointments, and calamities, and no matter how hard I try, that's where I consistently find myself, ass-down in a puddle of freak mud.

Or legs-up on an examining table.

During my visit to my doctor last year, a vital torturing device was missing, the little toy called the Speculum. For those of you not familiar with OB-GYN lingo, I will explain. The speculum is a medieval invention with two halves that, when closed, form a conical shape. That's the part they shove into your privates. Then I guess there's some sort of handle, and behind the handle is a big crank that, when the doctor turns it, opens the conical part to an unnatural spread resembling the jaws of an infuriated crocodile. It is made out of metal, and I'm pretty sure that my doctor keeps hers in the freezer.

During my exam, my doctor didn't find out that the speculum was missing until I was naked and already had my feet up higher in the air than an adult entertainer. She searched frantically for the instrument through the cabinet below me, but to no avail. It simply wasn't there. I thought I might have been off the hook.

Instead, she raised her head through the valley of my legs.

"Barbara!" she yelled to her assistant at the front desk. "Where's the speculum?"

"It's in the cabinet!" I heard Barbara yell back, to which my doctor responded that it just wasn't there.

Then the door flew open, and there was Barbara, entering the room to join my doctor in the search for the tool.

"I don't understand it," Barbara said. "I know I saw it here."

I couldn't see what was going on. I was still on my back, with my unsheathed lower appendages up in the air, my privacy covered with nothing but an enlarged two-ply paper towel.

"It's not here," I heard them agree. "Jeanie!"

And then the door opened again, and there was Jeanie, the girl in charge of the urine samples. She also joined the party that was currently being hosted by my now-public vagina.

"Look," I expected my doctor to say to her little friends as she elbowed Barbara and Jeanie and pointed at me, giggling. "I *told* you this one has seen a lot of action."

I felt like someone who had been abducted by a UFO, and aliens were handling me very improperly. "You people aren't supposed to be down there!" the little voice in my head yelled. "This is private property! Do you see an OPEN HOUSE sign?!!"

No one even offered to cover me up. I had no recourse; I just lay there, shaking my head. So far, I had my doctor, her receptionist, and the urine girl gathered in front of my very visible biblical parts. That included two people who had no business being there in the first place, both of whom I was going to have to look in the face later when I paid for this brief visit to Magic Mortification Mountain. What's next, I thought, a knock at the door and a voice that cracked, "Did anybody order a pizza?"

"Come on in!" the three women would chorus. "We're in here!"

Hell, let's send out invitations! Why stop with the office personnel? Let's have the whole building over for lunch!

Finally, my doctor sent Jeanie to the other examining room to fetch the speculum from that freezer, and the search was over. The examination proceeded, thankfully after Barbara and Jeanie went back to their desks.

So, you see, I'm wary of going to the gynecologist; I can handle it, but I'm cautious. But when I went back again this year, despite the public viewing I had last year, there was no way that I could have been prepared for what happened.

I went in, got the Pap smear/examination thing done, and it

was over. Everything went fine, no one walked in on me, no one strange poked at my private parts, and I didn't have to charge admission.

A week or two passed, and I hadn't heard from the doctor's office about the test results, so finally, I called them.

"Oh, Laurie Notaro, yes, we have your results back," Barbara said to me. "We lost your file, but we would have caught up with you by the end of the month."

Very reassuring.

"You need to come back in," she said. "When can we schedule a biopsy?"

"A biopsy?" I asked. "For what?"

"The test results are not okay," she said matter-of-factly. "You have abnormal cells, and we need to check them at the lab. It could be cancer."

Cancer? The word my family only whispers because it's too horrible to say?

Cancer?

Suddenly, I felt very mortal.

"Oh," was all I could say.

"How about next Tuesday at 2:30 P.M.?"

"Uh-huh. Sure. Yeah. Fine," I responded.

I hung up the phone.

This is wrong, I thought, this is *wrong*. I'm still a kid. I just turned twenty-two—okay, so that was seven years ago, but, still, I'm not that old.

Until I remembered that my cousin had a double mastectomy at twenty-five and that a friend of mine had developed lung cancer at twenty-four.

I had the biopsy done—which pretty much meant that my doctor cut a piece of meat out of me the size of a New York strip—and waited for Barbara to call with the results.

I started making plans.

If I'm going to die, I thought, I'm going on a shopping spree on my mother's credit cards, I'm going to Europe on pity money I can suck out of my dad, I'm going to eat Hostess Nutty Ho Hos for every meal and lose weight at the same time, I'm going to drink Hershey's chocolate syrup right out of the can, I'm going to smoke three packs a day and drink whiskey until I pee blood. Plain and simple, I'M GOING TO HAVE FUN.

Then Barbara called, and Europe was off. I didn't have cancer. It turns out that my cervix was just pissed off because I'd spent my prime childbearing years hanging out in bars, falling down, and vomiting on myself instead of making my womb ripe with baby fruit.

And, oh, by the way, I needed surgery, too, to get rid of the renegade cells.

Was next Tuesday fine?

Yeah, sure, fine, okay.

I went back to the doctor's office again to have cryosurgery, which meant that the bad cells were going to be frozen and killed, as Barbara had already explained it to me.

What I didn't expect was to see a huge iron tank set up next to the examination table that looked like my doctor was going to fill me up with enough helium to fly me over the Macy's Thanksgiving Day Parade as the Jolly Vagina Float.

Instead, the doctor explained that it wasn't a helium tank

but a liquid-nitrogen tank, which is what she was going to use during the surgery.

Oh, great, I thought. What happens if she's had too much coffee, or has a hangover and her shaking hand slips and then all of a sudden I have a freeze-dried uterus that shatters as soon as something comes into contact with it?

"Just relax," the doctor said.

I tried.

She turned on the tank, and I didn't want to do anything but snap my legs shut, *fast.*

She started the surgery, I heard the whirl of the machinery, and then I heard

BOOM!

from the tank.

Oh-my-God! My mind snapped into alarm mode. Frozen Uterus! Frozen Uterus! It didn't shatter, it blew up! My uterus has exploded!

"Ooops!" the doctor said.

That was NOT what I wanted to hear.

"It broke," she said simply.

"Which part?" I asked, meaning my fallopian tubes, the cervix, a vulva or two, which part was probably hanging out of me, dripping my eggs onto the floor?

"*Which part?*" I demanded again.

"This thing," she said as she showed me a circular piece of black rubber.

"That's not mine," I assured her, shaking my head. "It's not mine. I've never stuck anything that looks remotely like that up there."

"It's a part of the tank," she informed me.

Thank God, I thought, that my innards hadn't rotted to that sort of blackened stage just yet.

"We may have to reschedule," she sighed. "I don't think I have an extra part, but let me find out."

I nodded.

"Barbara!" she shouted.

Dead in a Box

To say that the middle bedroom in my house was messy was putting it mildly.

Some people called it the Scary Room.

Some people said it made a midwestern trailer park after a tornado look like a parking lot fair.

Some people said that they were sure that I hid dead bodies in there.

Those people weren't all that wrong.

The Scary Room came into existence the minute I moved into the house almost eight years ago. It was the first place that I put all the stuff that didn't have a rightful place already. It was the home for all of my orphaned possessions: the stuffed animals mummified with drool and snot from my childhood, the new wave albums from my teenage years, and all of the things my cat had ruined by peeing on them.

The Scary Room also became a storage facility for my two sisters, friends, and various roommates as well. The room became so full that movement within it was simply impossible; you could open the door, step inside, and look around. Anything else wasn't feasible.

Then, after seven years, the unthinkable happened: A light-bulb blew out, and the orphaned crap became nothing but towering, spooky shadows. Unless I had an out-of-body experi-ence or suddenly learned how to fly, there was no way that I could get to the fixture, which was in the center of the ceiling, to change it.

It wasn't until I was fired from my job that I decided I had enough time to tackle the project of changing the lightbulb. I started on a Saturday, fully determined to have an empty room by Sunday night.

Each box that I opened, looked through, and put in the trash pile was another voyage for the Ghost of Laurie Past. Some-times it was downright horrifying. In one box alone, I found an old pair of my underwear, a former boyfriend's GED diploma, a petrified cat turd, and a bunch of bounced checks.

I started running into the old, crappy furniture part of the Scary Room, so I dragged it outside and taped FREE signs all over it. Within an hour, the Dad-of-the-Month family down the street had this month's dad drive his truck two houses down to load up all the stuff and drive it back two houses to unload it.

After the furniture had been disposed of, I hit a crap pocket filled with all of the abandoned remnants of the last room-mate. As I was dragging the boxes to the trash pile, I noticed one little brown box that looked familiar. I remembered what it was and hoped that I was wrong, but I knew I wasn't.

It was a dead woman.

Or, more correctly, the mortal remains of a dead woman.

Apparently, the woman had lived at a resort where the for-mer roommate in question used to work as some sort of servant, and the two became friendly. The woman, who was very wealthy, died, however, and had no family to speak of, so her estate was left to a charity or something like that. A short time after she died, the former roommate found a box bearing her name in the hotel trash, while the label on the box read "Valley of the Sun Funeral Services." The former roommate, in the single act of compassion of his entire life, took the box home with him that night.

And now it was in my Scary Room.

I was raised a Catholic. We bury our dead people. *Whole.* I had no idea what I should do with the box. I couldn't call my mother. She'd have the Pope over to my house in fifteen minutes, armed with a cooler of holy water and an economy-sized crucifix. Whatever the right thing to do with the box was, I knew that the wrong thing was to let my house become its final resting place.

I couldn't throw it away with the rest of the stuff; it was bad enough that someone had thrown her away once already. My sister suggested that we hide the box in a drawer of a dresser that we were going to sell at a garage sale the next weekend, but that didn't work, because nobody bought it. My friend Jamie mentioned that we should slip the box in with the stuff that was going to be picked up by Goodwill the weekend after the garage sale, but I decided that that would be a bad idea. The box was too easily traceable back to me, and the last thing I needed was the Boomerang Box of the Dead popping up in all areas of my life.

So the box, now known and referred to as "Evelyn," remained on my kitchen counter in a very literal state of limbo. It was suggested that we bury her in the cat cemetery part of the backyard, but the thought of my dog having a strained movement over poor Evelyn seemed a fate worse than the Scary Room.

I thought about spreading her someplace, but I had no idea where. Where do you sprinkle a dead rich lady? At Tiffany? A nice lunch place? The shoe department at Neiman Marcus? Her cosmetic surgeon's office?

And besides, *who* was going to spread Evelyn? Did a priest, rabbi, or pastor need to spread her? Did we need a permit or license to do it? Were there fines for illegally dumping human remains, and how much were they? Could I do jail time?

I didn't know. I didn't know what to do or who to ask. All I knew was that I was trapped in a very dead version of a Woody Allen movie.

This went on for weeks, and I asked every person that I came in contact with what they thought I should do. My mother found out about it and disgustedly mentioned, "You know, things like this don't happen to normal people. That's what you get for letting weirdos live off you. It's just not normal."

And then I met Mary, the clairvoyant, at a coffee shop, while I was with my friend Michelle.

What the hell, I figured.

I told her I had a problem.

I told that I needed help.

I told her about Evelyn.

Mary nodded her head, took a breath, and said, "Well, what do you think the box wants you to do with it?"

I had no idea. I had held the box on several occasions, and I hadn't received a message from Evelyn in any of those situations.

Since Evelyn hadn't expressed to me what she wanted done, Mary asked what I wanted to do with the box.

I knew what I wanted to do. "I want to mail it back to the bastard who brought it to my house in the first place," I replied.

"That's exactly what you should do, then," Mary agreed.

"But I don't know if it's legal to mail the dead," I answered, and Michelle mentioned that she'd check it out with a lawyer friend of hers.

"But there's one thing," Mary added. "It's very important that you tell the box what you're doing and why. You have to tell her that it's not because you don't want her, it's because she needs to be where she belongs."

"Okay," I nodded, a little hesitantly, trying to picture the scenario and trying even harder not to laugh.

"Then as soon as you have the talk, get that thing the hell out of your house. You're playing with cosmic fire."

So the next day, while I was waiting for Michelle's phone call to see if I could slap a stamp on Evelyn, I put her box back on the kitchen counter.

I made some coffee and pulled up a stool.

We had ourselves a nice talk.

"You know, Evelyn," I started. "I like you and everything, and I've never charged you rent for the year and a half that you've been here, but—"

Then I noticed it. That's when I noticed that the Valley of the Sun Funeral Services label had been slit on either side of the box. I picked Evelyn up. I looked closer. The lid wasn't on so tight.

I had to do it.

I shook her. God forgive me, but I shook a dead woman. I shook her a lot.

And I didn't hear a thing.

Now, I know that ashes don't weigh much—in fact, they weigh close to nothing at all—but I knew damn well if the ashes of a whole, entire Evelyn were in there, I would have heard them settle somewhat.

It made perfect sense.

The former roommate found the box in the trash. Evelyn had been gone long before that, maybe floating in a clean, blue lake, or tangled up in a gust of wind that charged through the branches of a pine tree, but most likely lying in a big, fancy urn. Everyone knows that no matter how big of an asshole you are, you'll go to hell for throwing away a dead person.

But you *won't* go to hell for throwing away *the box* that the dead person was in just before their ashes were spread somewhere. If Evelyn was indeed a wealthy woman, I'll bet money that she had an expensive lawyer that made out a fancy will, complete with instructions on what to do with her remains, which were probably sitting in a porcelain urn on a marble mantel with a spotlight on it at the headquarters of her favorite charity.

I'll betcha a million dollars.

I didn't wait for Michelle's phone call; I didn't need to. Evelyn was going to where she belonged: back to the bastard who brought her to my house in the first place.

I just put the box in another box, wrote down the address, and gave it to the mailman.

What the former roommate didn't know—and didn't figure out when he got what he thought was Evelyn—wasn't gonna hurt him.

But I know one thing for sure.

Eight stamps never made me laugh so hard that I'd tinkled a little in my pants before.

I hope they never will again.

How Much It Costs for a Room of One's Own

Martha Stewart told me that I needed my own space.

She insisted that in a single afternoon, I could create a private and productive environment for myself by picking a spot somewhere in my house and tailoring it to fit my needs. She showed me how by transforming a mud room off her kitchen into a spectacular office, and, in a single afternoon, she painted the office, stenciled it with gold leaf, refinished the floor, and built a wooden wall unit from trees she had planted that morning.

I'm not a fool; I realize that Martha Stewart has the magic of television on her side, but in a quiet turn of contempt, I decided that I could do whatever she did. She wasn't better than me. I could create an office in a single afternoon, too. If I felt like it, I could make window shades from twigs and canvas. If I had a chainsaw, I could also sculpt a Nativity scene from a block of ice and make a delectable strawberry shortcake out of sawdust and a pound of confectioners' sugar.

Competition is healthy, as is jealousy to a certain extent, but it wasn't that as much as it was Martha's overall tone of voice.

It was a tone of condescending perfection, almost to the point of mockery. She seemed concerned, but was she really? Did she really feel that it was important for me to weave a carpet from my dog's fur, or was she just being a show-off? Would my self-esteem really rise if I rented a steamroller and paved my own driveway, or was she just being a know-it-all? Why was I watching her show, anyway?

Well, I *knew* why I was watching her show: I was out of work, and I have cable. That wasn't the only reason, however, there was more to it than that. I was connected to her. Believe it or not, I'm almost related to her.

It's true, by an odd and disturbing set of circumstances. You see, I have a distant cousin who was the niece of the husband of my father's sister whom I have never met. In fact, I'm not even sure if she *is* my cousin, but it enhances the story better than if I just said "some girl I heard of." In any case, this cousin graduated from Vassar with some degree and then became employed as Martha Stewart's personal assistant. Now, if you think I'm about to expose some horrible disfigurement about Martha's personality—like maybe that she picks her nose when she drives or leaves skid marks in the toilet—you're wrong. Nope. What I'm about to expose is that this distant cousin of mine allegedly became romantically entangled with not Martha but Martha's husband, a dead ringer for an ugly Aristotle Onassis. If that wasn't bad enough, Martha's husband left Martha, divorced her, and then allegedly married this distant cousin of mine, after which they honeymooned in Europe for three months.

Now, my aunt, the one who told me this story, is known to

exaggerate a bit, but I'm fairly sure that it's true. Sometimes I don't even *care* if it's true. I just feel lucky that I can pity Martha on some level.

And that's what I kept in the back of my mind when I decided in a single afternoon that the former Scary Room was the perfect spot for my new office, as I tore up the shag carpeting, swept away the spiderwebs, and threw away the dead lady I had recently found in there. I slapped the first coat of periwinkle-blue paint on the wall and it splashed back into my eye, causing temporary blindness. After an hour of flushing my eye with warm water, I went back into the new office, ready to resume my work, but it was dark outside. The sun had set. The single afternoon was over. Oh well, I figured, does it really matter? So I couldn't pull it off in a single afternoon, so what? Martha Stewart is still divorced.

The next day I finished painting and started on the floor, pouring adhesive remover gel on the concrete to eat away at the remaining carpet glue. However, what Martha didn't mention was that it was pretty necessary to wear the proper attire, like a NASA space suit, when using such chemicals, because the remover was equally effective at dissolving flesh as it was at dissolving glue. This was apparent when I noticed, out of my remaining good eye, that the gel had eaten a quarter-sized hole in my pants and was now gnawing through my calf muscles. Oh well, so what, I figured. So what if I had chemical burns that really demanded medical attention, if not a skin graft, did it really matter? Martha Stewart was *still* divorced.

After the floor was done, I set out to find office furniture, especially a great big desk. At the first place I went to, a man with a huge scab on his head led me through a maze of warehouses filled with rusted and dusty cabinets and tables. The first desk he showed me was it; a huge, 1930's golden-oak detective's desk big enough to sleep on. I loved it, and when I voiced my concerns about fitting it through the doorway of my new office, Scab Head told me not to worry. He assured me that his delivery men were experts at this sort of thing. They could fit any-thing *anywhere*.

I bought the desk.

Two days later, a delivery truck pulled into my driveway, and the two "experts" got out. They didn't look like experts to me as much as they did convicts out on work furlough. I swore I heard the theme to *Sanford and Son* drifting through the air. They unloaded the desk, grunting and moaning, and carried it to the front door, where they rammed the corner of the desk into the door jamb and gashed it.

After fifteen minutes, and with the use of pen and paper, the experts finally figured out how to get the desk through the front door. My faith in Scab Head's men was definitely waning as they carried it down the hall and toward the new office. I already knew what was about to happen.

They turned the desk on its side and tried to slide it in. Didn't work. They moved the desk upright and tried to bring it in at an angle. Didn't work. They took the door off its hinges and tried to bring it in again. I knew that this maneuver wasn't going to work when one of them asked me if I had a saw.

"Where is your second choice to put the desk?" the other one said.

I took a deep breath. "There is no second choice," I answered. "This room is my personal space."

"We don't have the authorization to help you any further,"

one of them said. "We don't have the allowance from our boss."

I was getting mad. "It was your boss that told me not to worry about this," I mentioned. "He said you were experts."

"Yeah, but we don't have the authorization," he said again, as if that explained everything.

"Oh. Well, how am I supposed to get this in there?" I asked them as they began to put the door back.

They shrugged. "See, we'd have to call and get the authorization, you know, so we could spend the extra time to get it in there, but we just don't have it," the expert explained to me.

"Have what?" I asked.

"The authorization," they said together.

"Stop saying that and go. I'm giving you the authorization to get out of my house. Just go," I almost screamed. "You know where the front door is. It's the first big wooden thing you put a dent in."

And they left, and I watched them go as I stood next to the desk in the hallway.

I knew what Martha would do.

I took the door back off the hinges.

I took out the drawers and used a screwdriver to pry off the top of the desk.

I turned the desk on its side and pushed and wiggled and pushed and wiggled until the desk was in my office underneath the window, and my spine was popped so far out of alignment that it nearly broke the skin.

Hunched over, I put the top back on and screwed it in place. So what if I couldn't stand up straight? Who cared if I couldn't walk anymore? Big deal if I was in agonizing pain.

I know what Martha would have done.

She would have bought herself a truckload of painkillers with her big, fat alimony check and drunk gin until she passed out, like any sensible divorced woman.

I wish I had an alimony check.

For the Birds

The truth was that I felt sorry for the two little girls from down the street, Casey and Staci.

I don't know, maybe I'm a sucker; maybe I'm just too gullible. Nevertheless, I must still hold tight to the theory that a six-year-old child at my front door asking me to feed her because her mother hasn't gotten out of bed in two days qualifies for a Sally Struthers kind of tragedy.

I had met the girls a couple of months ago when they, one of them fully dressed as a ballerina, wanted me to pay them to cut my bushes, though I politely declined. My regular gardener was a forty-year-old man who equates a properly trimmed bush to a stump, and I knew I wouldn't have much more luck with an eight-year-old and a six-year-old.

After the bush incident, the kids started coming around in the afternoon, and, within a week of our meeting, it had become a daily ritual. The chimes would be tinkling, yet no one was visible through the front-door window. That's when I knew the midgets, as I started to call them, were getting hungry.

But soon, feeding them simply wasn't enough. They started

bringing their dog to my house for Snausages and dinners of Kibbles and Chunks. Every time they set foot through the front door, one of them would spot something she liked, pick it up, and ask, "Can I have this when you die?"

This begging thing was obviously either a genetic trait or a habit picked up from their mother's fourth husband. One day, while disposing of all the unnecessary items in our house, I came upon the dusty, 1973ish fakewood headboard that had belonged to my sister's old boss. Somehow, after the boss's father had died in the bed, we assumed possession of it. I was quite ready to get rid of it, so I dragged it out to the front yard, slapped a huge FREE sign on it, and waited for someone to pick it up.

Within a half hour, the headboard was spied by the fourth husband, whom I call "Jethro," while en route to dropping both Casey and Staci off at their natural fathers' homes for the weekend. He sent the midgets up to the door to tell me to take the sign off the headboard while he smoked a cigarette at the end of my driveway.

After that, I came up with a whole bunch of ideas to trick Jethro. I toyed with the idea of dragging all of my trash, lawn clippings, and broken appliances to the curb and taping FREE signs to them so I wouldn't have to take them all the way to the Dumpster in the alley. Jethro, however, had beat me to the punch by hauling a plaid burlap love seat with missing cushions out to the dirt plot that was his front yard, appropriately accompanied by a broken dryer. As a matter of fact, Staci had been missing for several hours one afternoon until I saw her older brother open the door to the dryer and yank her out.

I bet, I thought to myself while driving past their house, that if I moved the dryer and the love seat to my yard and put FREE signs on them, the fourth husband would take them back inside the house.

I just hoped that they'd move soon, but they couldn't have moved soon enough. Last Sunday morning, the doorbell rang, and as I peered from the hallway to the front door, no one was visible. It was the midgets, probably wanting breakfast.

Despite the fact that I was still in my pajamas, I opened the door, hoping to get rid of Casey and Staci quickly, but as I did so, I knew I had been trapped.

There they were, dressed in the same clothes as the day before, but this time, on top of Staci's right shoulder was perched a big, fat, filthy, dirty pigeon.

I shuddered immediately. I avoid birds, I avoid them at all costs. I've never had a simple, noneventful encounter with a bird and never will because of karma. I killed a bird with my car several years ago, and since then, birds have been shitting on my head, getting trapped in my air-conditioning vents, and being generally bothersome. To me, seeing a bird is like seeing the Antichrist appear before my eyes.

"You're not bringing that thing into my house," I told them right away.

"This is Petey. He broke his wing, and we're taking care of him. See?" Staci said, stretching out the bird's wing so I could see just how broken it was.

"Then he needs to be at your house resting," I said back.

"Isn't he pretty?" Casey said, stroking the bird's head.

"Nothing is pretty if it carries more vermin and disease than rats," I informed them. "And that's what pigeons are: big, fat, flying rats that shit—I mean, *poop*—on people's heads. Now take it home, girls, and make sure you wash your hands with gasoline."

Reluctantly and saddened, the midgets turned around and headed back down the driveway with Petey. I headed into the kitchen, ecstatic that I had successfully slipped away from a bird unscathed.

Within moments, I heard screaming from outside. As I listened closer, it was the terrified shrills of the midgets, calling my name over and over. As much as I wanted to ignore their cries for help—as much as I wanted to plead the case of "I'm Not Your Mother, So Go Drag Her Drunk Ass out of Bed"— I opened the side door and voluntarily, although quite hesitantly, surrendered myself to the Midgets' Lair of the Filthy Pigeon.

I didn't want to go outside.

There was danger outside.

Simply concerned that the pigeon had turned mad and had plucked out one of the girls' eyeballs, I rushed outside to the front yard, where both girls were burrowed under the bougainvillea bush.

"Help us, Laurie, help us!" Casey screamed. "Petey got away, and he's under the bush! We need to cut it down!"

"Uh, no, we don't," I replied, crouching down until I could see the bird underneath the bush, moving around and spreading his vermin about. "First of all, stop screaming. Now, one of you get on the other side and we'll flush him out."

Staci ran around to the other side, tunneled under her

end of the bush, and immediately shrieked, "PETEY! PETEY! PETEY!" which naturally caused the bird to quickly scuttle over toward my direction. Against my better judgment, I caught it.

"Here," I said, thrusting Petey at Casey. "Here's your bird. Now go straight home and keep him there."

The girls gathered him up and started home. They weren't one step out of my driveway when they began screaming again, and I turned around just in time to see Petey, in a desperate waddle, escape out into the street.

Both girls began to cry hysterically, and their yelling became even more high-pitched when they spotted a car eight blocks away.

"AHHHH! He's gonna die! He's gonna die!" Staci kept yelling. "LAURIE! You have to help us! Oh, NO! He's gonna die!"

Suddenly, there I was in the middle of my street, wearing a T-shirt and no bra, and striped pajama bottoms and barefoot, hunched over, chasing and trying to capture a filthy bird that I hated. The more the girls screamed, the faster the bird waddled until I was almost breaking into a jog behind it, my arms outstretched and my boobs flopping around, completely unharnessed.

For two blocks, I ran after the bird down the middle of the street as he desperately ran for freedom or the next best alternative, the car. I couldn't blame him. I, too, would have gladly thrown myself in front of a speeding vehicle if my destiny rested in a shoebox located anywhere in that family's house. Casey and Staci ran slightly behind me, hollering and howling, tears shooting down their faces.

Finally, I cut the bird off, forced it in the opposite direction and corralled it back into the yard belonging to my most dangerous neighbor, Frank.

Frank, in a pathetic attempt to deny that Christmas was indeed over, although it was now February, still retained his handcrafted holiday finery in his yard. This included a barrage of plywood Santas, Snoopys, snowmen, and elves with yellow eyes. Frank informed me that he had electrically wired his yard with enough volts to "knock a horse on its ass" in an effort to thwart potential thieves from stealing his decorations. I knew the capture had to be cautious to prevent electrocution, and I spotted Petey hiding between two gargantuan reindeer.

I made the only safe decision I could.

"There he is, girls!" I yelled, pointing. "Go get him!"

They both dove in between Donner and Blitzen, and wrestled Petey as his broken wing sadly flapped in a fluttering panic.

"We got him!" they both yelled as they jumped up.

"Good job!" I nodded. "Now take him home, quickly. Run. And if you ever bring another animal to my house again, I'm calling the foster care people."

I didn't see the girls again for a week. Then the doorbell rang; it had to be the midgets.

When I opened the door, they both looked sad, their faces long and their eyes drooping.

"What's the matter?" I asked them. "Is Petey okay?"

"My dad said he got better and flew away," Casey said.

And I bet you guys had "chicken" for dinner sometime this week, I thought.

"We're moving today," Staci said. "We're leaving at lunch-time for our new apartment."

"We wanted to say good-bye and give you a hug," Casey said. "We're going to miss you."

If I had been premenstrual, I probably would have cried. I did feel bad, though, and I wondered what the hell was going to happen to these kids, but I already knew. Each of them was probably going to have four or more kids by different fathers by the time they were twenty, just because they didn't know that their lives could have been any different. There was nothing I could do about it, anyway.

"My mom has a magazine with your picture in it," Staci said. "And we're going to keep it so we can look at you."

"Really?" I laughed.

"Yeah, and I decided something," Casey said. "I think I want to be a writer someday. Just like you."

What the hell is this? I thought. Am I trapped in some *Hall-mark Hall of Fame* movie? Who wrote the script for this? Danielle Steel? If God wanted to put a lump in my throat, why didn't he just hit me in the neck with a softball or a brick instead of making little kids do his dirty work?

I had no choice but to let them in the house, where I proceeded to give them everything they asked for, even though I wasn't dead yet. I had to get a grocery bag because they wanted so much stuff, including a dusty old seashell, smelly soaps, a can of tomato soup, and a stick of margarine.

"Thank you," Casey said. "But we have to go now."

"We have to get ready for the new apartment," Staci added.

"Well, remember one thing," I told them. "When you guys

get to be twelve, and your mom asks you what you want for your birthday, you tell her you want—now, can you remember what I'm going to tell you?"

They both nodded.

"You tell her you want Norplant. Okay?"

"What's Norplant?" they asked.

"It's insurance," I answered.

With their bags of my household possessions slung over their shoulders, they left for home. In three months, I knew, they wouldn't even remember who I was.

I wish *I* was that lucky. To remember them, all I have to do is look down the street into their front yard to see the burlap couch and the dryer their fourth dad had left behind.

Waiting for
the Bug Man

We were waiting for the bug man.

Again.

This was his second visit to our flea-infested home, since whatever it was that he'd sprayed around the first time possessed the killing power of an aromatherapy candle.

But we still liked Fred, our bug man. He was a simple fellow, short, squat, with skin color that indicated he was one quick, vigorous motion away from a stroke and teeth that looked like Indian corn.

Our first introduction to Fred was delayed by seven hours, since he didn't arrive for our 9:00 A.M. appointment until the sun had officially set. I had completely given up on him, taken off my bra, and was picking at my face when I heard a knock at the door. His forehead was an oilfield bubbling with sweat. Salty puddles gathered at the points where his thick trifocal lenses rested on his cheeks in cracked, dry, brown eyeglass frames. His face took on the appearance of a genetically enhanced strawberry, except for those corn teeth, and he was breathing as if he had just left a porno theater.

"Would you like something to drink?" I asked, trying to be kind. "I have iced tea, water, or I could make you some Kool-Aid."

"Yep, sure," Fred speed-stuttered. "Need somethin' cold."

"Okay," I said, opening the cupboard and reaching for a glass. "I'm out of ice, but everything's been in the refrigerator. Is that okay?"

"No," Fred said quickly. "I need something cold, I'd better have something cold, I shouldn't drink nothin' hot."

"Oh, it's cold," I assured him. "I just don't have any ice."

"No, no," he said as he shook his head. "Better stick with something cold."

Okay, I thought, realizing right away that my experience with Fred was just a spontaneous freak encounter. Fred apparently had his problems—he indeed had some issues on his plate—but far be it from me to provoke a weird, stuttering stranger in my living room who happened to be holding a big tank full of poison.

So I showed Fred where we were having our flea problems, and he began pulling the trigger to his canister. I retreated to my bedroom when I got a long-distance phone call from friends on vacation that I needed to pick up from the airport the next day.

As I was taking down their flight information, I felt a tap on my shoulder, and as I turned around, I saw my boyfriend and Fred standing behind me next to the bed.

"Honey," my boyfriend told me, "Fred needs to use the phone."

"Right now?" I mouthed. "I'm on long distance."

"He says it's an emergency," he explained.

Okay, I thought, maybe my flea problem is so extensive that Fred needs to call for backup, or maybe he's spilled something toxic in my house and needs to call a biohazard SWAT team. I ended my call and handed him the phone.

He dialed. "Hello," I heard him say. "It's Fred."

Silence.

"*Fred.* Fred the exterminator. I'm running a little late. I wanted to call and let you know. Okay. Bye."

My boyfriend and I looked at each other.

"That's an emergency?" I asked.

"It must have been his ten o'clock appointment," he replied.

Fred hung up the phone, finished spraying around the house, and then left without even saying good-bye. Just jumped in his truck and drove away.

But the fleas didn't.

As soon as he walked out the door, complete familial colonies of fleas that had been in temporary hiding sprang out of the living room carpet and bit our ankles, executing bitter revenge, and it didn't stop there. I've never been bitten in such private places by anything that didn't at least pay for dinner first.

A week later I couldn't take it anymore, and I had to call Fred to come back. I scheduled the appointment, again, for 9:00 A.M.

We didn't expect him to be on time, we really didn't. We decided to spend the day waiting for Fred and watching TV trash talk shows.

The doorbell didn't ring until *Oprah* was on, which made

Fred a typical seven hours late. It was OK. I kept my bra on and left my face alone. I was ready for him this time.

I opened the door, and Fred was oozing bodily fluids.

"Come on in, Fred," I motioned. "I have ice for you."

I poured Fred a big glass of iced tea with four Sweet'n Lows, and as he gulped it down, I could tell that there was something different about him. His teeth were still brown, but I could see all of the nubs he still had. He was smiling. Fred had taken to us.

He was amazed that we were still having flea problems and ran out to his truck to get a special canister of potent insecticide that would "actually kill them this time," he said. I could hear the gust of powerful spraying as he pointed it at the couch.

When Fred was done in the living room, he came into the kitchen and stopped in his tracks when he saw our dog.

"You know," he said to my boyfriend, "it ain't legal, but my son asked me to spray his dog when he had flea problems."

I thought he was joking. "Oh, we don't need to spray her," I laughed. "We're just going to burn the fleas off of her with a blowtorch after we dip her in gasoline."

"Well, I'll tell you," he informed us, his eyes steadily glued on our whining Labrador, who was obviously sensing Fred's dishonorable intentions. "After I sprayed that dog with a good coat of Diazinon, the flea problems were gone."

"That's because a dog needs to have skin before it can have fleas," my boyfriend said in disbelief.

"All right then. Suit yourself. I guess I'll spray in here," Fred said, and my boyfriend and I decided to go elsewhere in the house to leave the man to his work. We brought our dog with us, just in case.

We went back into the bedroom and smoked until Fred started on the hallway and bedrooms. It seemed to be taking a while, but we didn't want to rush him, so I flipped through a magazine, my boyfriend picked up a book, and we smoked some more. I had gone through the entire magazine, and Fred still hadn't finished in the kitchen.

"Go see what he's doing," I said to my boyfriend. "Maybe he finally inhaled too much and has gassed himself or swallowed a loose corn tooth and choked to death."

He got up and quietly went down the hall, then turned around and came right back.

"He's all right," he said.

"Is he done spraying?" I asked.

"I don't know," he said.

"You don't know?" I pressed.

"He's sitting down," he explained. "He's watching *Oprah*."

"He's watching TV? Fred is watching TV? Do you think he's retarded?" I whispered. "Because I think he's retarded. That man is retarded."

"He's not retarded," he insisted. "He can't be. He drives a truck."

"Oh, yeah," I nodded.

So we waited until *Oprah* was over, Fred finally finished spraying, and he left without saying a word. Just got in his truck and drove off.

It wasn't over. I knew I was going to have to call him as soon as the fleas came back in an hour. That is, until I looked at the canister sitting on the kitchen counter, full of the potent spray stuff that Fred had just left us for absolutely free.

I gasped. I was so excited. The stuff was straight from the manufacturer, which meant no dilution, no sparse spraying. It meant no more fleas. No more bites. No more itching. No more scabs, only cancer!

I cried I was so happy. It made my heart jump every time I thought about it. A flea-free life sounded so beautiful. I planned to spray everything on my next day off. It felt like Christmas.

Until the next day when the doorbell rang.

It was Fred. He looked sad.

"Hi, Fred," I said as I opened the door. "You're late! *Oprah* was over fifteen minutes ago!"

"I lost my bug spray," he said lifelessly. "Did I leave it here?"

"NO," I said, trying to be a good actress.

"I'm pretty sure I left it in your kitchen," he added. "You didn't see it?"

"NO," I expounded.

"I really need it," he expressed. "I need to find it. Will you call me if you find it?"

"Yes," I said, without offering him anything to drink.

I shut the door. I flew back to the bedroom, where my boyfriend was waiting, after he'd hidden the canister under the bathroom sink.

"I can't keep the bug spray, can I?" I said sadly.

"Who are you kidding?" he replied. "I know you already made plans to meet Jeff and Jamie by the Skin Pit when you get to hell."

"Fine, I'll give it back," I pouted. "But not before I've had my crack at it."

I took the canister from below the sink and headed into the living room, aimed and pulled the trigger, keeping my finger firm and determined until I had sprayed enough that I was gagging and had to open every window in the house for ventilation.

Only when the gagging cloud had dissipated and cleared did I find my way to the phone to call Fred's exterminating company. I left a message saying that my boyfriend had found the canister, but had mistakenly identified it as hair spray—though the doctors were hopeful that some of his sight might return with transplants.

I did not feel good about telling on myself.

I did not feel that my conscience was clear.

I felt that I needed to spray some more.

I sprayed until my boyfriend yelled that I should at least leave *something* in the can for Fred, even if it was just a rattle, and that I was going to kill all of us with that stuff.

Well, he was right, at least partially. I did kill some of us, and for that, I'm glad.

I haven't been bitten by a flea since.

I Have a Note from My Mom . . .

On my diet that I started in 1977, I was starving and nothing was happening.

So when my friends Jeff and Jamie began mentioning that they were going to sign up for the fitness center at a local community college, I listened.

After all, I figured, the reason I never joined a gym was because of what was *at* the gym: big, bushy-haired blond girls with eighteen-inch waists and five-thousand-dollar bustlines. Thick-necked jocks wearing neon tank tops who grunted when they lifted things that were heavier than my house. People who had two high-fashion wardrobes, one for regular life and one for their gym life, clothes that they washed after they sweat in them.

I certainly couldn't deal with that. It would be just like high school, I imagined. Girls with perfect bodies lolling about the locker room, whispering that my bra had a Sears label hanging out of it and that my panties could double for a parachute, before they lined up for an impromptu Vegas-style kick dance, singing, "Who wears short shorts?"

It would be horrible. I hated PE in high school and paid the tallest girl in my class to forge a note with my mother's fake signature on it that read, "Please excuse Laurie from all future activities involving sweating, perspiring, or getting hot. She has extremely weak pores, and perspiration will send her into cardiac arrest. Her doctors are working on it. Thank you, Mrs. Notaro."

But the fitness center was different, Jeff and Jamie said, they had been there. It wasn't like PE at all. You didn't have to go into the locker room if you didn't want to, and there were no uniforms. You could do what you wanted for however long you wanted, and no one bugged you. The more Jeff and Jamie talked about the fitness center, the more I became convinced it was a good idea. Plus, I thought, if I went with my friends, it wouldn't be so bad. They were slugs just like me. We could all leave slimy trails on the fitness center equipment together.

So I did it, I joined. I was proud of myself as I made an appointment along with my friends for our evaluation and orientation session.

On the appointed day, I was late getting home from work and tried frantically to get ready for our first day at "my gym." Jeff called the minute I walked in the door to tell me that he'd pick me up in ten minutes.

I dug through my closet and found one sneaker without a mate. I grabbed a pair of leggings off the floor and threw them on, only to find that the seam in the crotch had ruptured all the way to my inner thighs. Shit. A T-shirt is what I needed, I thought, a long, big T-shirt to cover the hole in my precious parts. I spotted one in the hamper, flung it on, but it didn't come close to covering my map of exposed skin and unshaven areas. In the hamper, under the T-shirt, rested a pair of a former boyfriend's dirty boxer shorts. I hesitated for a moment, then snatched them, sprayed some Glade in the crotch, and I was suddenly poppin' fresh.

I still had to find my other sneaker, which I did just as Jeff pulled into the driveway. I put it on, grabbed a water bottle, and was out the door.

Our instructor hadn't been quite so diligent about arriving on time, however, so the attendant showed us into a small lounge area where we were to wait for him.

"Make yourselves at home," he told us with a healthy, robust smile.

"Okay, thanks," I replied. "Could you get me an ashtray?"

His eyes got real big and his mouth fell. "Uh" was all he said.

"She's kidding, she's kidding," Jamie jumped in as she shot me a dirty look.

The attendant's face returned to normal, then he left the room.

Jeff and Jamie *both* shot me looks. "You promised you'd be good!" they cried together. "We haven't been here for three minutes, and you've already gotten the blacklist ball rolling. We agreed that we wouldn't tell anyone here that we were smokers!"

"Fine," I said. "I didn't realize that it was such a mission."

After a while, our instructor came in, made us watch a film, and had us fill out a questionnaire about our health. After I answered all the questions, he looked at it, reached for my ID tag, and slapped a big black B on it.

"Um," I said, pointing to the letter of obvious shame on my card, "what's that for? Bulky? Behemoth? Biohazard? Babbler?"

"It's for your back," he answered, pointing to a section on the form in which I'd detailed the problems with my slipped disc. "You can't do the same things that the other people do. You need to work at your own pace, take things easy and slow."

What he was saying, essentially, was that I was special. I was different. I was in the slow group. I was going to be the last one picked for teams, just like in grade school.

Already I was the fitness center flop.

After all of our forms were filled out, another instructor, Brian, appeared to show us how to work the equipment properly. We entered the gym, and the very first thing we saw, the initial sight that we encountered, was a woman, although I'd rather call her a bunny. She was complete with perfect, flowing hair, a glowing, seamless tan, ripped muscles, and upper arms that didn't have a trace of the skin swag that swings when you wave at people. She wore a brightly colored, multipatterned shiny leotard with coordinating tights, socks, and wristbands.

"Hate her," Jamie and I said as we turned to each other.

Brian started us off on the leg push or pull thing, I'm not sure what it was, where we placed our feet on a pedal of sorts and extended our legs until we had lifted our weights. Jamie went first, and it looked pretty easy. Then it was my turn.

I got on the machine, put my sneakered feet where they were supposed to be, and I pushed. I watched my feet as I went push, extend, contract, extend, and that's when I saw it: a brown oval spot on my shoe, right at the very tip of it. I gasped at myself.

Cat poo. The cat had shit on my shoe—not that this had been the first time, but every time is equally as horrifying. I couldn't do anything at all, I couldn't do anything, except insist that the instructor show us how to use another piece of equipment that hid my feet.

"We can't do that," he explained to me. "You have to follow the order."

"Then I think I just pulled a hamstring in my knee," I added quickly. "If I continue in this exercise, I might need a lawyer."

He brought us over to the next piece and showed us how to use it. On this apparatus, we had to lie on our stomachs with our heels underneath a bar, which we had to bend our legs and lift.

Brian climbed on and off the thing with the skill of a pro, which I guess he was. So I tried it. The bench that we were supposed to lie on was waist high, too high for me to lift my leg over and straddle. I tried it. I looked like an old boy dog with a misplaced hip trying to pee into a kitchen sink.

"Try getting on from the side," Brian coaxed.

So I went to the side and attempted the climb, groping and pushing myself up and onto it, as he and Jamie watched.

"I can't do this," I told him. "I feel like I'm mounting a sea turtle."

He nodded. "Your friend told me that you thought you were a comedian."

There was no way I could do it, for me it was physically impossible unless I took a running start, circled the gym several times to build up momentum, and when I got to the belly-flop leg-lift thing, flung myself onto it.

"Let's try something else," Brian said, to which I agreed and picked up my backpack to move onto the next thing.

Suddenly, something shot out of the side pocket and went sliding across the floor, stopping only when it hit the tip of Brian's Nike.

A gold, half-empty pack of Camel Lights.

"So," he said as he picked it up and handed it to me. "You're smokers. Comedian smokers."

"*She* is!" Jamie shouted, pointing at me.

"Oh, don't be ashamed!" I snapped at her. "It's a cigarette pack, not a crack pipe."

"Might as well be," Brian sighed. "I don't think it would be a wise idea to attempt the StairMaster today."

"You promised," Jamie whispered.

"I'm also wearing some boy's dirty underwear," I shot back.

I should have made copies of that note from high school, I thought. I just should have made copies.

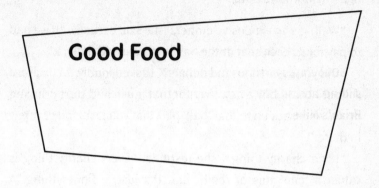

Good Food

I didn't want to go.

I didn't want to get dressed up, or do my hair, or put on eyeliner, or try to find a matching handbag.

I didn't care about meeting basketball star Charles Barkley.

I really didn't.

But my friend Sara did, and it was only at her insistence that I agreed to go to the dinner thing, even if I did have to wear something nice. It was a free meal at a hoity-toity hotel, anyway.

My friend Huck had invited us, having won a Phoenix Suns raffle. It was only a dinner, I reminded myself, an hour of polite conversation at best, and most likely, I'd get free dessert, too.

So I said yes to Sara, tell Huck that I'll go. After all, he was a good friend of mine, and I was flattered that he thought enough of me to ask me to be one of his guests.

Danny Manning would be sitting at our table, Sara informed me, and that was special. I nodded, even though I had no idea who she was talking about. Not all the tables had celebrity basketball players at them, she added.

"Well, it's an expensive dinner," she said casually. "If we had to pay for it, each seat at the ball is a thousand dollars."

"Did you say a thousand dollars?" I asked loudly. "*A thousand dollars?* I could buy a new liver for that much and start drinking again. And back up to that 'ball' part that you just kind of threw in there."

"It's a charity thing," she justified. "Every charity thing is called a 'ball' this or 'ball' that. It's just a dinner thing. A dinner-and-dancing thing. We get free Nikes, too."

"A dinner-and-dancing thing with a thousand-dollar price tag is a ball, Sara," I insisted.

"Okay, it's a ball, but it's too late for you to back out," she said decidedly. "Huck already RSVP'd for you, and Nike ordered your little shoes."

I knew I couldn't afford to buy a ball gown, so the next day I went to a fabric store, bought some taffeta, tulle, and organza, cut the velvet bodice off a vintage dress, basically stapled it all together, and I had a goddamned ball gown in which I was ready to eat a thousand-dollar steak. With a little deodorant and a lot of lipstick, I was as good as I was gonna get.

Hagarella was ready for her ball.

Sara picked me up, and we headed to the Arizona Biltmore, the fanciest resort in town. When we got there, we checked in, got our little Nike sneakers, and found our table. Huck smiled as he introduced us to his other guests, two sets of sisters that looked like twins to me. Twin Group A was a fortyish sister/sister duo decked out in more sparkly beads than the rear ends of two Crystal Water trucks, burning my corneas if any ray of light should happen to hit them from any angle.

Twin Group B, two bartenders from some fancy restaurant also in the Biltmore, exuded snot in their pink Ann Taylor suits and were obviously JUST TOO GOOD to talk to us. We hated them right away, and I think that came out when I repeatedly asked them what color apron they had to wear while performing their duties in the "service industry."

But I didn't care. I was there for my thousand-dollar steak, and I didn't care, even when the waiter dribbled beer on my head and lap and some wealthy woman stepped on my dress with her free Nike and ripped the shit out of it. Even when Danny Manning could not have given less than a rat's ass about providing his promised celebrity conversation, and the snotty bartender twins started giggling and then going to the bathroom with his wife.

When my steak came, it turned out to be a filet mignon, which I would have placed at a two-thousand-dollar dinner, and I dug in. It was wonderful, tender, flavorful, creamy if that's possible, and I savored bite after bite. I didn't notice as the Crystal Water Truck Twins downed carafe after carafe of white wine, and I didn't notice that, immediately after I had shoved a quarter of a yellow squash in my mouth, Charles Barkley was behind me, wanting to shake my hand.

I looked up, and there he was, his shiny head right near mine, and there I was, trying diligently to swallow whole a piece of squash the size of four DD batteries that I couldn't even manage to get my teeth over.

"How are you?" he asked as he extended his hand and I reciprocated. "Are you having fun?"

I nodded, with wide eyes, I'm sure, shaking his hand as he

waited for my reply, which was lodged right smack behind the squash. Squeezing itself up and over my gums and teeth, the reply was suddenly free, and it escaped in a muffled cry—since my tongue was pinned down by the massive girth of the vegetable. I heard the reply as it started, driving itself in slow motion to procure the clearest delivery possible.

"GOOD FOOD," is what I said.

"Good food" is what I said to Charles Barkley, "Good food" was my intelligent and witty answer, "Good food" was the product of the muse that twirled itself outside of my mouth.

GOOD FOOD?

A Bosnian refugee with absolutely no command of the English language could have come up with something better than that, I screamed silently at myself.

He looked at me slightly and tilted his head in a curious motion. Then he quickly withdrew his hand, as if he had suddenly realized my body was covered with weeping lesions, and moved on to one of the twins.

Stunned by my own inadequacies, I realized that I hadn't even used my tongue when I spoke.

"He thinks I'm retarded," I found myself saying aloud.

"Oh, how nice," he must have thought as he tilted his head, "that someone took the little retarded girl to the charity ball. I bet the ball is for her charity. I bet she's the poster girl."

"He thinks I'm retarded," I said again.

"No, he doesn't," Sara said, trying to console me. "He probably just thinks you have some little mouth deformity."

The Crystal Water Truck Twins, on the other hand, were having a grand time. One of them had kicked off her Nikes and was strutting around the dance floor like a stripper. The other one was too busy stalking Charles Barkley around the room, touching him in an overfamiliar way and trying desperately to get his attention.

She wanted his autograph, and with liquor fueling her determination, she marched to the nearest table and whipped five used napkins off of it, shoving them underneath both armpits. Then she walked up to an innocent woman and just plain snatched the pen out of her hand, all the while keeping her double vision on Sir Charles.

The dancing Crystal Water Truck Twin had apparently worn herself out and returned to the table, where she picked up Sara's wineglass and downed it. Her sister, on the other hand, was tapping Barkley on the shoulder like a woodpecker until he turned around. She presented him with the napkins and pen. He smiled politely, yet tiredly, and began scrawling on the dirty linens.

At the table, however, the second sister had disappeared, and I hoped it was to the bathroom, where a lot of cold water on her face would have done her a world of good. The snotty twins had long ago vanished after exchanging phone numbers with Danny Manning's wife and taking one last trip to the bathroom together, where I believe they shared a lip liner.

After she got each napkin signed, the sassy Crystal Water Truck Twin lassoed it around and over her head until she was swinging five of them, after which the basketball player kindly excused himself and rejoined his friends.

Suddenly, a loud disturbance from underneath the table exposed the dancing Crystal Water Truck Twin, who popped up quickly, smacked her hand on the table, waved, and said, "Hi!" with a giggle.

"You need to call a cab," I said with a slight sympathetic smile and a nod.

We weren't about to give them a ride, and I wanted to get the hell out of there before the bold twin found her car keys. I grabbed Sara, got our real shoes back, and headed toward the car.

The ball was over, and my thousand-dollar steak was now being churned and marinated in bile.

I checked the rip in my dress, and we began to drive away, fully wishing that I had hit that rich lady or at least threatened to sue her for ruining my original gown. I was just about to get really mad when I saw something sparkly and blue on the side of the road with what looked like maxi pads shoved underneath her arms, dumping the contents of the upside-down purse on the grass, obviously looking for keys. Beside it was another glistening figure, passed out cold and belly-up on the lawn of the Biltmore hotel.

I could only think of one thing to say.

"GOOD LIQUOR."

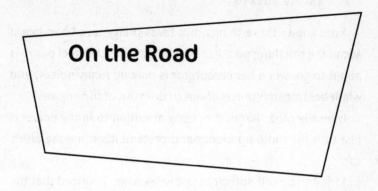

On the Road

I'll be brutally honest: I know nothing about my car.

I know where the ashtray is and I know how to pump gas. That's it.

If you try to teach me how to change a tire, I'll forget. If you show me how to check the oil, I won't understand. If you change the adjustments on the driver's seat, it will take me three weeks to figure out how to get them back. I'm just not that kind of car girl.

My friend Kate tried to help me by teaching me how to fill my tires up with air. I, of course, don't own a tire-pressure gauge, so she was particularly careful to show me the right way.

"You mean I can't just leave the hissing thing on the tire until the time runs out?" I asked quizzically.

"Absolutely not," she replied. "The tire will blow up on you."

"And take all the skin off my face," I said, nodding.

"No, no," she answered. "It will explode on the road, when you're driving. Then just pull over and call AAA."

"No, I heard it's okay unless they blow up in your face," I informed her.

Kate knows these things, but I was pretty sure I had heard about the tire thing on 20/20. She knows when her fuel pump is about to go, when her carburetor is making funny noises, and when her transmission is about to drop out of the engine.

I, on the other hand, don't pay attention to funny noises. I just turn the radio up louder and pretend it's someone else's car.

I tried to be self-sufficient last week when I noticed that the tires were looking squishy again. I dropped my quarter in the air machine, counted to thirty on each tire, and figured I was done. They looked big, full, and ready to go. My face was intact. Kate would have been proud. It was Monday morning, and I was heading down the freeway because Nordstrom's was having a shoe sale, and I had to be there first.

I was making the curve at the busiest portion of the freeway when I heard a terrible noise. A horrible, grinding sound that started at the front of my car and filled my ears. It was far too loud for the radio to drown it out, no matter how high I turned it up. I knew right away what it was. 20/20 was wrong.

Kate was right. Tires *do* explode on the road, I thought.

I remembered her words and pulled onto the shoulder as hordes of cars whizzed by. I carefully got out to see which one was gone, but as I walked around the entire car, I was surprised to see that they all looked okay.

I got back in the car and started it again, convincing myself that it really had been someone else's car making the noise, not mine. I hit the gas, and immediately, the sound returned.

Oh Christ, I thought, what is it? What happens when your transmission drops out, the clutch goes bad, the fuel pump quits? I had no idea. I called AAA on my cell phone and told the operator that I needed help.

"Do you need a tow truck?" she asked.

"Maybe," I answered. "What happens with a bad transmission? I think that may be the problem."

"You won't be able to go into drive or reverse," she said.

"Okay. Then how about a bad clutch? I think that may be the problem," I mentioned.

"Do you drive a stick shift?" she responded.

"No. Okay, what about a fuel pump? I think that may be the problem," I said, panicking.

"I'm just going to send a truck, lady," she said.

"I'm just not a car kind of girl!" I pleaded as she hung up.

Ten minutes later, I jumped when someone knocked on the passenger window. It was a cop. I had forgotten to put my hazard lights on, mainly because I don't know where they are. I lowered the window. I know where that button is.

"Hi," I said quickly, "it's my fuel pump. Or transmission. Or carburetor. Or muffler. I think it's my muffler. I've called a tow truck, it will be here any minute."

"I don't think you'll need a tow truck, ma'am," he answered. "You ran over a gas can."

"Oh," I replied.

"How far did you drag that thing?" he asked. "I don't know how you didn't see it. It's as big as a TV! Do you have a jack?"

I hoped to God I did, and that he knew what it looked like.

I popped the trunk (I know where that button is, too) and helped the cop take out a couple of lamps, a box of books, and a pile of dirty clothes I had forgotten were in there. I was embarrassed when he found the jack, put it in place, jacked up the car, lay down on the ground, and then kicked the biggest gas can I had ever seen out from underneath my car, but not as embarrassed as when he got up just in time to see a big gust of wind from a passing truck rush toward me and blow my skirt all the way up to my chin.

"Your tow truck is here," he said, trying not to laugh.

Are You the Petersens?

I was biting into the best tortilla of my life at my favorite Mexican restaurant when I saw her.

Sitting at the next table, behind my friend Jeff's head, there she was: my eighth-grade math teacher. I couldn't mistake her still jet-black hair, the soft curve of her almond-shaped eyes, and her thin, pursed lips.

It was her, all right.

I nudged my friend Jamie, who went to all the same schools I did since the third grade, and was now sitting next to me enjoying her very own heavenly tortilla.

"That's my eighth-grade math teacher!" I said to her as she lifted the buttery, golden, nearly transparent tortilla up for another bite. "Do you remember what her name was?"

"Was that the teacher that made you stand in front of the class and add fractions until you cried?" she asked for the benefit of Jeff and Kristin, our newly betrothed friends who were sitting on the other side of the table, since we didn't meet Jeff until high school.

"That's the one," I confirmed. "She's also the one that gave me detention for asking why we couldn't just 'round up.'"

"You got in more trouble then than when you stole all of those *Little House on the Prairie* books from the library, and the librarian caught you with *On the Banks of Plum Creek* stuffed down your pants," Jamie added.

"They weren't pants, they were Sassoon gauchos," I stressed. "And I *had* to steal them. I didn't have enough baby-sitting money to pay for the late fines on that *Joanie Loves Chachi* book that I found stuffed in my little sister's Easy-Bake Oven two years later. I still can't believe gauchos went out of style."

"Her name is on the tip of my tongue," Jamie finally remembered. "Her husband was my biology teacher in ninth grade . . . Mrs. Petersen!"

"MRS. PETERSEN!" I nearly shouted.

"And that's him right there!" Jamie pointed out excitedly. "Mr. Petersen is sitting right next to her!"

"You guys should say hi," Kristin said. "I'm sure they would like to see you."

"I don't know," I said, shaking my head. "I wasn't the best student . . ."

"I know!" Jeff ventured. "Maybe you can impress her and completely validate her career as a teacher if you show her you can figure out how to leave a tip!"

"Why didn't you guys *both* have her for math?" Kristin asked innocently.

I looked away.

"Well, you see," Jamie started to explain, "in junior high, I was in a special group for math and science."

"What do you mean, 'special group'?" Jeff practically yelled. "Do you mean . . . you were in the Dumb Group in math?"

I turned my eyes back to Jeff. "It's NOT called the Dumb Group, Jeff!" I hissed. "It's called Essential Math Skills, and it's nothing to be ashamed of. Some people have more creative skills than technical skills. Some people want to smell the flowers instead of counting the petals! Some people are just circles being hammered relentlessly into square peg slots! Some people just want to ROUND UP!!"

"I was in advanced-placement math," Jamie finished.

"And I . . ." I said quietly, "was in . . . Slow Math."

The silent pause at the table was timeless and dreadful.

"Somehow," Jeff finally stammered, "I now see you differently. Do you . . . get checks from the government? How did you get a driver's license?"

"If you fill in C for every answer, you're bound to get some right," I snapped.

"I still think you should say hi to them," Kristin repeated. "Won't Mr. Petersen be thrilled to know that Jamie is now a microbiologist with her own cancer research lab! And Laurie, you didn't need math after all to write . . . those little things in the paper! See? You should say hi!"

"I still don't know . . ." I hesitated, shaking my head.

"Come on." Jamie nudged me. "I will if you will!"

"Oh, all right," I said, giving in.

"I have a microscope and an autoclave in the car," Jamie said, jumping up from the booth. "Should I bring them in?"

"I don't have any of . . . my little things," I protested. "That's hardly fair."

Slowly, we took the two steps necessary to reach the Petersens' table, where Mrs. Petersen had her lips stretched wide to accommodate a rather thick taco. Mr. Petersen, on the other hand, was armed with a fork and knife, and was preparing to bludgeon his chimichanga.

"Excuse me," Jamie said, leaning over slightly.

The Petersens suddenly froze in time as they looked up at us.

"It's Laurie!" I said as I waved at Mrs. Petersen. "Remember me? 'Round up'!"

Mrs. Petersen's eyes grew wide; her mouth was still open, though slightly more circular, as if to accommodate an element of complete horror.

"LAURIE NOTARO!" I emphasized, sensing that she could not place me. "From Retard Math! I write little things for the paper now!"

"It's Jamie," I heard my advanced-placement friend say to Mr. Petersen. "Remember when we cut open that cow's eye, and Mike Purcell ate the retina on a bet, and you made him throw up in the sink?"

"Want me to figure out how much you need for a tip?" I said to Mrs. Petersen. "'Cause I can!"

"I have slides and a microscope in the car, but she wouldn't let me bring them in," Jamie said, and added in a whisper, "She was in Retard Math."

The Petersens remained silent, saying absolutely nothing as they just sat and stared at us.

"Um," Jamie finally said. "Are you . . . the Petersens?"

The two of them slowly, and in a synchronized movement, shook their heads from side to side.

The fake Mrs. Petersen pointed at me. "You have refried

beans on your cheek," she said, still holding her taco with her other hand.

We took the two steps back to our table as the fake Petersens continued to gawk at us.

"You won't believe this," Jeff said as we slid back into the booth, "but your high school English teacher is sitting right over there!"

"Mrs. Gaio?" I said as Jamie and I both turned around to look.

"It's her, all right," Jamie said.

Revenge of the Bra Girl

I was searching for a slip in a major department store not very long ago, perfectly content to mind my own business. In the lingerie department, two teenage bra girls were busy rehanging a mountain of bras they had culled from the dressing room fifteen minutes before closing.

They were working as fast as they could, making small chitchat between them as they tucked straps back onto plastic hangers.

"You guys are having a clearance sale, huh?" I asked, as they nodded with something of a scowl. "I know all about it. I used to be a bra girl myself."

As a former bra girl, I have seen more mammary glands than Larry Flynt.

When I was a lass and got thrown out of college for the first time, my parents came up with a plan: I had to get a job.

I applied at a large department store, got called for an interview, and instantly had visions of myself parading through the dressing rooms dispensing invaluable critiques to malnourished, size-six fashion junkies: "Lose that caboose!" "Are those your upper arms or honey-baked hams?" "That little paunch tells me you're in the wrong department, mama. Maternity is on the second floor." But instead, the human-resources director looked at me and said, "What luck! We have an opening in lingerie!"

Bras and girdles. My vision switched gears and reminded me of my first bra fitting when I was ten and my mother felt that my "lentils" (a scientific term she used for not-yet-developed bosoms) were beginning to sprout. Before I knew it, I was in a dressing room with an elderly saleswoman's hands cupped over my niblets, categorizing my size as a "grape on its way to a lime." As I tried the bra on, she scooped her fingers inside the cups to make sure that the grapes had ample room to mature into big jugs of wine.

"And one other thing," she garbled as she opened the door to the dressing room. "You'll be a woman before you know it, and if you leave all of that black spaghetti under your arms, it will give you cancer!"

After I was hired at the department store, however, I discovered that when adult women enter a lingerie department, they become primitive, unbridled beasts. They see it as a sanctuary where they may absolutely unbutton their shirts, feeling no shame or reserve, and flash a salesperson while saying, "Do you have this bra?" They feel that it's completely acceptable to bring twenty bras into a fitting room and leave the nineteen that don't fit on the floor and draped over doors, none of which are on a hanger. They also find it appropriate to approach an eighteen-year-old bra girl while they are practically naked and ask, "Can you hook me up?" "Do you think this is a turn-on?"

and "This tummy tucker is too tight, and I need help getting it off!"

I also saw men purchasing lurid, sexy teddies in a 36DD and a petite-size flannel nightgown at the same time, saw women leave their dirty bras and panties for me to find while they walked away wearing new ones, and once I even caught a trailer-park couple diddling in a fitting room and got to call security.

The lingerie department, in short, was like the devil's playground. All morals melted away like chocolate as soon as the customers spotted an Olga tag. Probably the very worst part of the job was that I always got in trouble for chitchatting while I was rehanging a hill of bras before the store closed for the night, and explaining that I was working at the same time put me on employee probation.

All of that psychological damage was brought back as I watched the fingers of the two bra girls fly furiously between straps and hangers. I was paying for my slip when, like a bear charging through the woods, a short, stocky woman with a silver pageboy shoved a rack of body slimmers out of her way and pointed at the girls. "Maybe if you'd stop talking, you'd get some work done!" she roared at both of them, and then narrowed her appetite down to one. "YOU! Come with me! I'll give you something to do!"

The poor bra girl put down her current project and followed the bear into the maze of robes.

"Now we're never going to get this done," the surviving bra girl sighed. "That manager, Eileen, is so mean! She made a girl cry last week because the Wonderbras weren't hung in alphabetical order."

I felt sorry for the bra girls because I understood only too well. I nodded. Then I had an idea.

I grabbed my bagged slip and headed out into the forest. I circled the entire sales floor twice with eagle eyes, finally stopping at the Fashion Passion department.

"Have you seen a mean rhinoceros of a woman with a silver pageboy haircut scurry through here?" I asked.

Both of the salesgirls shuddered. "You mean Eileen," they said. "We just heard her howling in Fancy Pant-sy, but we'd stay away from her if we were you. Word has it that she bit a salesgirl in Houses of Blouses, and she hasn't had her shots."

"That's exactly why I'm here," I said, and headed off in that direction.

I saw the silver goblin turning a corner, and I couldn't let her get away. "EILEEN!" I shouted, and she immediately stopped and turned around.

"Can I help you?" she asked with a sudden smile.

"Yes, you can," I said in my best adult voice. "I was in lingerie when you yelled at that salesgirl."

"Yes, well, those bra girls can sure chat up a storm," she laughed. "All play and no work! Ha-ha-ha!"

"You're wrong," I said sternly. "Bra girls are hard workers. Every last one of them. They see horrible things, are forced to touch the inhuman, and have to be nice to fat, near-naked women and their breasts. They are faced with insurmountable odds every day, because they all know that bras NEVER hang themselves up. As soon as you hang one, someone else tries it on and leaves it on the floor. It's like working in a sweatshop!"

"Well—" Eileen started.

"I'm not done," I interrupted her. "And those two girls were talking, but they were working at the same time. Some people are talented enough to do that!"

"I—" Eileen tried.

I held up my finger.

"Still not done," I continued. "Because you were wrong, Eileen. You were wrong to accuse them, and you were wrong to yell, and as a customer of this store, I demand that you go back to the lingerie department and give those girls an apology!"

"I didn't realize," Eileen said, obviously shamed. "I will do that."

Eileen turned to go.

"And one more thing, Eileen. Do you have this bra?" I asked, pulling open my shirt.

A Hole in One

I'm pretty sure that it had been my favorite tooth.

It was a solid tooth, white and strong and sturdy; a squat little tusk, located perfectly as the last in a line of other squat little teeth in the upper right side of my mouth.

I thought the tooth liked me, too. I did everything I could to be kind to it, I bought it chocolate and gum, and rubbed my tongue over it every now and then to express my love.

But being kind to something doesn't necessarily mean that it won't revolt someday, and may do so in a manner that causes blood to spill until it's dripping down your chin onto a bib.

I wasn't doing anything particularly nasty when the revolution began; I was eating gummi bears and watching TV when the tooth decided to liberate itself and broke off in several sharp, thin splinters. At first I didn't understand what had occurred—it felt like I had bitten into a dirt clod or a piece of gravel—but when I spit out the candy, I saw the carnage right away.

My heart skipped a beat, and the first thought that popped

into my head was, A splinter of glass in a gummi bear. That means early retirement and a life of leisure for Miss Laurie Notaro after the personal-injury lawyer takes his cut.

But as I looked closer to see exactly how solid of a case I had, and if I'd be living in a villa in France or a mobile home in Branson, Missouri, I noticed something heartbreaking. The shard of glass was white and ridged. As I began to recognize it as a former body part, I understood that half my tooth was broken, split, and embedded in the orange-and-red chewage, and I was in trouble.

I've had dreams like this, dreams in which my teeth felt loose, and with one poke of the tongue, the tooth dropped out of my gums like a brick from a rotted foundation. I've had dreams in which numerous teeth fell out so quickly that I collected them in my pocket and kept my mouth shut to prevent more dental abortions, though my mouth eventually felt like it was full of small pebbles.

I panicked. With my most horrible nightmares coming true, my anxiety level started to rise, making my skin cold but my insides burning hot. So I decided, quite quickly, that my plan of action would consist of what I do best.

I was going to ignore it.

There's a simple reason for this, as my mind flashed back five years, back to the last time I had visited the dentist. I had possessed a molar that rocketed straight through the cavity stage and lodged itself in pure and total decay, which ultimately resulted in a nasty abscess that froze the left side of my head in a throbbing ache.

I went to my mother's dentist, who examined the tooth

briefly and told me I had one option: the tooth needed to be pulled, and as he stuck his hand back into my mouth and took a firm hold on the tooth, I understood that he meant NOW.

I didn't have time to actually think about it, let alone give an answer before I felt an enormous pressure on the lower half of my jaw, where the doctor—who I now believe did his internship at Auschwitz—was yanking.

He was pushing so hard that I really thought my jaw was going to snap in half, and as I tried to be brave, a baby-sized tear rolled out from beneath each closed eye. The pressure stopped.

I opened my eyes.

The doctor was looking at me, his hands on his hips, and his mouth twisted in a grin.

"So," he said with his head cocked to the side, "we feel like being a crybaby today, do we?"

I was in such shock after this comment that I didn't even bite down when he plunged his hand back in my mouth and pushed even harder.

"Well, we're halfway through!" he taunted.

I decided right there and then that I'd rather pull the tooth myself with a steel-link chain and a trailer hitch and was ready to shoot out of the chair when he laughed and tossed something in front of me on the silver tray. When I looked down I saw it was my tooth, covered in blood, roots and all, and I realized that the animal had ripped it out with his bare hands.

I had been orally manhandled.

I gasped then but laughed six months later when I saw on

the evening news that the bastard had signed a lease in the state pen for five to fifteen for tax evasion, substance possession, and intent-to-sell charges. Sticking his entire hand in my mouth and wrenching a tooth out of my head was kitten's play compared to the talents of his new neighbors.

So, by ignoring my newest dental/gummi bear catastrophe, I was following my own best advice, and I followed it faithfully. I stopped chewing altogether on that side, didn't drink on that side, and was very careful with my toothbrush.

I ignored it for quite a while, until it started to pinch me every now and then, until the pinch evolved into a pulse, the pulse into a throb, and the throb into shooting knives of pain. I knew I had to do something and most likely do it in a hurry. I mentioned the situation to a coworker, who suggested that I might need a root canal to save the tooth, and then went on to document the procedure, which included drilling, screws, needles scraping the inside of my tooth, and, finally, some type of molten lava.

It didn't sound pretty. In fact, it sounded worse than having my tooth ripped from my jaws by the bare hand of a convict, but when the ache reached my eyes and my neck, I called my mother's new dentist.

They rushed me in immediately, offered me headphones for a CD player or for the TV, which was turned on to *The Sally Jessy Raphaël Show*. This is a dentist's office? I thought to myself. I didn't hear anyone moaning or sobbing in pain, and I finally came to the conclusion that I must be at the rich folks' dentist.

The two dental assistants, Mimi and Gigi, dressed in identical outfits and wearing name tags in the shapes of molars, introduced themselves and began taking X rays. The doctor finally came in and started poking around. He looked at the X rays and gave me my options, which I already knew. I could have the tooth pulled, which naturally brought back horrible memories, or have the combination platter of root-canal-and-crown procedure, which might require some additional surgery to some bone in my mouth.

"Which one do I get knocked out for?" I asked, trying to weigh the pros and cons.

"Neither," the dentist said. "But I'll give you nitrous oxide if you get it pulled."

"I hope you have an Incredible Hulk grip!" I decided. "Get that thing out of my head!"

So I opened wide, the doctor positioned his tooth-puller tool, and I breathed in deeply from this artificial-heart-looking contraption that Gigi or Mimi put on my nose. It made me happy, though I could feel my tooth sliding downward. Meanwhile, Sally was interviewing a man who accused his ex of being a tramp, telling the audience that "she had more things stuck in her than a porcupine has stickin' out," but before the ex even had a chance to respond, the dentist stuck something in my mouth and told me to bite down.

"All done," he mentioned happily.

As happy as he was, I was ecstatic.

"Ah duh?" I reiterated defectively, due to my gauze-packed mouth and my novocained lips that made me feel like I had just had a stroke.

The gentle dentist nodded and showed me the shell that

used to be my tooth, all cleaned up and tidy, to which I burst forth in a spray of indiscernible gratitude babble which meant, "You, my dear sir, are no dentist! You are an artisan! A magician! A wizard! And if you give me pills that I need to show an ID to pick up at the pharmacy, I will totally be a character witness at your trial!"

He looked at me oddly, half-smiled, and handed me a prescription.

"It's codeine," he told me. "And with codeine, you need to take it with—"

"Wee-wee!!! Wee-wee!!!" I said, in my best attempt at *whiskey.*

"—food," he finished.

Well, I thought to myself, no one's funny with a yard of gauze in their mouth and the lips of a dead woman.

"Give this girl some oxygen," he said to Mimi or Gigi. "I'll be financing her early retirement if we let her drive home like this."

So Mimi or Gigi made me sober up by inhaling a lot of oxygen, which I really didn't want to do. In fact, at that point, I didn't care if they had torn out every tooth as long as I could keep breathing from the tank. I'd even get my legs waxed if that stuff came in the kit.

When I got home, I waited a little while before I dared do it. I waited until the blood clotted a little and, more important, until the double dose of codeine I had taken kicked in.

I ran my tongue along the gum where the tooth used to be, above and behind, and finally, in the fleshy, wet hole that used to be the nest of my favorite tooth.

"Let that be an example to you," I said to the surviving teeth. "If any of you has any ideas about acting up, just look at the hole. Any more bad behavior and you're *out*. No second chances."

That's how we treat revolutions around here.

Waking Angela Up

Until six months ago, I'd never lived in an apartment. I didn't know what it was to hear my neighbors flush a toilet, do their dishes, or talk on the phone. But when I went to Tucson to start a new job, I moved into a tiny place and became immediately aware that I was not alone.

My neighbors downstairs, affectionately known as "the Trolls," were partial to loud, passionate arguments. They swam in the pleasure of standing in the breezeway at five in the morning, fighting about which one of them had the keys to the car, or banging on the walls with a heavy object to really put their point across.

So I was relieved when my landlord said that their lease wasn't getting renewed because they "looked like drug people." Who doesn't look like drug people? I said to myself, but I was just glad they were leaving.

I had almost forgotten about their departure when someone knocked on my door last night. I nearly didn't answer it—no one comes to my apartment without calling first, because you can't get in the building unless you have a key. And, besides, I wasn't wearing a bra.

But as I shuffled toward the door, my nose dripping from allergies, curiosity got me and made me turn the doorknob.

And there she was.

"Hi," she said awkwardly.

I nodded.

"Is this the back apartment?" she asked. "The apartment in the corner of the building?"

I nodded again.

She was tall. Thin. Tan. Blonde. Cute black glasses. Short, spiky haircut. Shaved legs.

"Oh, okay," she continued. "I just moved in. I'm your neighbor downstairs. I'm Angela."

No you're not, I thought to myself. You're Uma Thurman. And me, with a tissue pressed against my left nostril, a cigarette in my other hand, my permed, frizzy hair that I cannot control, and no bra—well, I'm Janeane Garofalo. The Truth About Giraffes and Water Buffaloes. I immediately felt inadequate.

She was the AntiLaurie.

"I, um . . . I keep a late schedule," she started (because I'm sure she's a model, my brain snapped), "and I guess you get up at eight?"

"Seven," I shot back. "I have a job."

"Well, in the morning . . . I guess because of the wood floors, when you walk across the room, I can hear it."

"I'm on a diet," I said defensively. "I'm trying to lose weight."

Angela paused. "It's when you wear high-heeled shoes. They make a lot of noise. Could you wait to put them on until you get in the hallway?"

"Do you want to fight?" I knew I should have asked her. I could have totally taken her down to the parking lot and fought her. I'm spunky and quick, and hate gives me the strength of a monkey.

Instead, I said, "Sure," even though Angela's schedule was no more important than mine; even though my true friends would say that I was super-cuter than she was; even though I felt as if I were in seventh grade again, and the head cheerleader had just come over to me in English class and told me that I was in her seat and was making it hot and sweaty.

Angela smiled and bounded down the stairs, but I didn't let her off so easy. I yelled back, "You're lucky I don't drink anymore, Prissy Pants!! I would have punched you! Tomorrow morning, you'll be waking up to my version of *Riverdance!*"—right as the door closed behind her.

I know. I was embarrassed. "Prissy Pants" just flew out of my mouth.

Back inside my cavernous, echoing apartment, I walked around on the wood floors, mouthing to myself and pointing at no one in particular, "Late schedule, huh? Well, I was the Queen of the Late Schedules, you little snit! Who do you think made up the Twelve O'Clock Rule? That was me! That was ME!!!" (I pointed to myself at this part.)

"That's right! If I made it home before seven in the morning, it was an early night! My day *started* at Happy Hour!! We used to call it Happy Breakfast! How do you like THAT, Little Miss I-Keep-a-Late-Schedule! You don't know what a late schedule is! AMATEUR!"

This morning, when I woke up, I was a little bit calmer. I tiptoed across the living room and headed for the bathroom. Once situated, I stopped in a panic. If Angela could hear me walking around, she could hear every loud noise I made. I turned on the faucet for background noise and tried to go, but I couldn't, knowing that Angela could hear any splashes or torrential wee-wee downpour.

I couldn't turn on the TV, afraid that I'd wake Angela up. I took a trickle of a shower in case the water was too loud and I'd wake Angela up. I drank cold coffee because I thought that the beeps of the microwave would wake Angela up. The only thing I could do in quiet was smoke. I was pretty sure that wouldn't wake Angela up, unless the smoke seeped through the floor and set off an alarm.

Finally, in a burst of bravado, I used the hair dryer, but only for a second. I set my shoes out in the hall, got my backpack and smokes, and headed out the door.

Out in the hallway, I squeezed one shoe on and then the other, and started to get my keys out to lock the door.

Suddenly, from the open back window of the apartment, I felt it reach my frizzy hair before it came shooting toward me, and I just stood and watched as the wind ripped through my apartment with both hands outward and slammed that door shut, hard enough to rattle the glass panes in it, hard enough to scare the pigeons off of the windowsill, hard enough to wake the dead.

I smiled, turned around, and skipped down the hall.

Angela's Revenge

There was a knock at my door.

A little, petite knock, almost as if maybe someone didn't want me to hear it.

"Someone's at my door!" I whispered into the phone to my friend Dionne, who had called in between Must See TV shows to tell me some gossip. "I'm not going to get it!"

"Who do you think it is?" Dionne whispered back. "Do you think it's—"

"No!" I almost shouted. "No, it couldn't be her! I bought slippers! I got them from Nordstrom's clearance rack for three dollars. They're pink with bows, and I could only find two left feet, but I've been quiet! It can't be Angela!"

Angela, my perfect, beautiful downstairs neighbor had recently come up to my apartment to tell me that my galloping across my living room floor like a donkey was waking her up in the mornings. Since then, I'd bought the slippers, learned to read Katie Couric's lips while watching the *Today* show, and waited until I got to work to go to the bathroom, so that no walking, TV noise, or toilet flushes would disturb Angela from her very unneeded beauty rest. Dionne knew all about Angela, because I had dragged her to a million thrift stores to find an "Angela Rug" for my living room to muffle the noise, and because I had written a column about the whole thing.

Looking through the bottom panes of my French front door, I saw someone put something down in front of it and walk away.

"They're gone!" I whispered to Dionne. "They've left something in front of my door! I think they're gone!"

I put down the phone and raced to the door, unlocked it, and swung it open far enough to launch the offering, now identified as a plant, out into the hallway, spilling soil everywhere.

The knocker was not gone. She turned when she heard me and came back toward me as I crouched, attempting to scoop up the dirt with my nonsmoking hand. As she passed into the light, I knew my mistake was fatal.

It was Angela, naturally, you knew it, I knew it, Dionne knew it. If it was possible, she looked even better than she did before, in a checked mini-suit, black knee-high boots, and a cute little purse.

"Hi," Angela started. "I just wanted to thank you for being so quiet. I know we got off on the wrong foot, and I just wanted to give you something to say thanks."

"Oh. That's cool. I got slippers," I said, pointing to my two pink left feet.

I was already aware that, if possible, I looked worse than I did the last time. Again, no bra, my chi-chis tossing about like a car in a Tilt-A-Whirl ride. My Ted Kaczynski/Unabomber hair was flying all around my head, before Dionne called I had picked at my face, my eyeliner remained black smudges on my cheeks because an ash had flown into my eye on my way home from work, I was smoking, and I had a mammoth Count Chocula cereal and milk stain on my T-shirt from dinner about the approximate size of a kidney. I looked like Zelda Fitzgerald, right before the BIG fire.

"You always catch me at my best times," I added with a little staged, nonchalant laugh, when what I really wanted to say was "Can you hang out here for, like, thirty minutes, because I am almost cute, and I can prove it," "Do you want to come in and see my clothes?" "From down here, I can see that booger in your nose," or "You're an adult entertainer, aren't you?"

But I didn't say anything, except thanks, as she handed me a card. I took my blotched face, destroyed self-image, and new little plant inside. "I'm going to kill you," I whispered to it.

"It was Angela, wasn't it?" Dionne questioned me as soon as I got back on the phone.

"Yes," I answered sorrowfully. "I'm not wearing a bra again, and I messed with that pimple on my chin that you told me not to. And she looked like a Prada ad."

"Did you show her your clothes?" she asked. "What did she leave by your door?"

"A stinky plant," I answered. "And a card."

"Read it," Dionne insisted.

As I flipped the envelope over, I noticed that Angela had written my name on the front. "Dionne, this is odd," I said. "No one spells my name right, no one. My *grandmother* never got it right. But Angela did."

"How could she know?" Dionne replied. "There's no way. Unless she saw it somewhere. On your mailbox?"

"No, there's just my apartment number. Where could she have seen it? Unless she read . . ."

"Unless she read that column you wrote about her," Dionne said simply. "You rock, sister!"

"Not so hard, Aretha," I said, looking down. "My pants are on inside out."

All Smut
and Perverts

My mom got e-mail.

"I need your Internet address," she announced when she called me. "Want to be my cyber pal?"

A sudden chill cut through me straight to the bone.

A pal, with my mom? On the Information Superhighway? My mom, akin to electronic technology? Are apes running the world, too, now?

Not too long ago, she was fascinated one day by a new, bright red light that kept flashing in her kitchen. "I think your father bought this for me as a surprise," she whispered as she showed it to me. "Can you believe they make microwaves this small now?"

"That's your answering machine, Mom," I said. "And that message must be important, because you've programmed that thing to let the phone ring forty-six times before it picks up. Wanna hear it?"

"Nah," she said, "if it's really important, they'll call back."

"Oh," I said, "I bet it's the phone call I made to you when

someone was trying to break into my house in 1995. You should listen to it, it's a good one. I cry on it and everything."

She also has call waiting that is nothing but a wicked myth on her cordless phone.

She bought a VCR that requires a drum roll, an ancient chant, and a sprinkle of fairy dust just to turn on.

And now she was playing with e-mail.

"Mom," I said as gently as I could, "the most technical thing you've ever done was to give your credit card number to a QVC operator over the phone, and that's only if call waiting doesn't beep in. You can't even control the appliances you have now. Figure out how to work the camcorder first, and then we'll move on to e-mail."

"I can do this," she asserted. "I'm going to get the Complete Internet Book for Dummies."

"Well, while you're at the bookstore," I added, "pick up the Total Internet Guide for Idiots, the Absolute Internet Guide for Jackasses, and the Entire Internet Book of the Dead. That should do you."

"Don't get fresh," she warned me.

A day later, I got an e-mail.

"Hi, Laurie," it said, "it's Mom. I bet you didn't think I could send you an e-mail. I'm not real crazy about QVC on-line, I'd rather watch it on TV. Don't forget to e-mail me. From, Mom."

Two hours after that, I got a phone call.

"Are you mad at me?" my mother asked. "Why haven't you e-mailed me back? I've been waiting!"

"I didn't have anything to say," I confessed.

"Then say *that!*" she said, her voice rising. "I love it when the machine says, 'You have mail.' It makes me feel like Meg Ryan!"

I felt a dark precedent coming on. I could see my mom using the Internet to do all of her Mom's Dirty Work, because in the realm of my mom's e-mail world, I was *mute*. It was her dream, a dangerous, magical dream. I quickly imagined being barraged by her e-mail messages, saying things to me without the potential to even talk back to her.

"Hi Laurie. It's Mom. Clean your filthy house. From, Mom."

"Hi Laurie. It's Mom. Go to church or go to hell. You choose. From, Mom."

"Hi Laurie. It's Mom. Shave your monkey armpits or you're going to find yourself single again. From, Mom."

"Hi Laurie. It's Mom. Why don't you answer my e-mails? From, Mom."

E-mail, however, wasn't the only Internet frontier my mother wanted to conquer. After watching *The Rosie O'Donnell Show*, she called me again.

"What's eBay on the Internet?" she wanted to know. "Is it ebonics for something dirty, because I don't understand it."

"Remember the Internet auction I got addicted to last year?" I asked her. "That's eBay."

"I want to do the eBay," she said sternly. "Rosie does something on it for charity. I want to help. As long as it's not pornographic or a perverted chat room. I don't want anyone putting my head on a naked body like they did to Sophia Loren. I don't get my kicks that way. Will you come over and help me do the eBay?"

"Only if you show me the naked picture of Sophia Loren," I replied.

"Don't get fresh," she warned.

So I went over to help, and logged onto the site to register her. "You need a user name," I explained. "What do you want to use?"

"Not my *real* name," she cautioned. "I don't want anybody knowing who I am. I watch *Dateline.* I know people can get your address and start sending you . . . things. I know someone is going to try and put me on the Internet naked. Those things happen, I've seen it on *Dateline!* The Internet is all smut and perverts!"

"Mom," I said, trying to reason with her, "it's not like some old man is going to mistake you for a sixth-grade boy and offer to buy you a bus ticket to Orlando, Florida. It doesn't work that way. You don't just turn on your computer and then proceed to run through a gauntlet of sex offenders."

"What would your father say if his friends saw me on the Internet naked?" my mother shot back.

"They'd probably be nicer to him, but it just doesn't happen like that," I said. "I'd be giving away snapshots of myself if I really thought someone would paste my head on a naked Pamela Anderson and put it on a website. Kodak couldn't process enough film. Go ahead, take my head, terrorize me with it. If someone put a picture of my foot on a naked Pam Anderson, I'd be thrilled, let alone a part of me that could be identified."

She shot me a look, then thought for a long, long time. "Um . . . Cory! How's that for a name?" she finally said.

"Your dog?" I said as I typed it in. "I don't know, Mom. *Entertainment Tonight* might pick up on that. Well, it's taken anyway. Pick something else."

"How can it be taken?" she argued. "Cory is *my* dog! I want to use that name! I need something I can remember!"

So then she made me enter the names of all the dead dogs we've ever had, like Bambi, Pookie, Ginger, and Brandy. "This is dangerous, Mom. You've been subconsciously naming your pets after strippers," I said, but she just ignored me. "You'll be a pervert magnet."

After we learned that those names were also all taken, she agreed to the next available "Cory" name, which was "Cory34."

"Now just how am I supposed to remember that?" she asked, still pouting. "I'm going to have to change the dog's name! 'Want a cookie, Cory34?' 'Look, Cory34 made a doody on the floor.' Oh, yeah. That sounds smart. Just show me Rosie's stuff!"

I clicked on the Rosie pumpkin head, and a new screen appeared with the charity auctions. When my mother got a good look at what was up for sale, she threw down her mouse and balked.

"Rosie's out of her fat little head if she thinks I'm paying a thousand dollars for Madonna's autograph!" she said in disbelief. "I don't even *like* Madonna! That's not help! I'll *help* somebody, I'm not above that, sure, here's five dollars! But this? That's like asking for a kidney! Get me off of this thing! You stop laughing at me, Laurie!"

When I went home later that night, I checked my e-mail. I already knew what the message said before I opened it, but I clicked on it anyway.

"Hi Laurie. It's Mom. If you write a column about this, I'll kill you. From, Mom."

The Candy Apple Freak Show

"Sun's up," my friend Jamie said as she, our friend Krysti, and I zoomed down the highway last week, heading for Pasadena and a day of shopping. "Time to eat!"

I was starving, too, and my appetite was for a big, fat candy apple that I always get in Old Town Pasadena when we go there. It's the best candy apple in the world. First, they dip a beautiful green apple in gooey, homemade caramel, then they dip it in white chocolate, roll it in Oreo cookie bits, AND THEN they drizzle *more* white chocolate all the way around it. It's heaven on a stick, and the only thing that could make me love it more would be if it were laced with Fen-Phen.

The vision of that candy apple kept dancing in my head, all gooey, crunchy, and nearly nutritious because of the apple part.

"I'm getting a rumbly in my tumbly," I hinted. "There's a candy apple in Old Town just calling my name! I can feel it."

Jamie and Krysti just looked at each other. "Forget it," they almost said in unison. "When we do get to Old Town, you'd better not get any big ideas about eating it when you're standing next to us. We don't want to be a part of your Candy Apple Freak Show!"

I gasped. "I thought I could trust you!" I cried. "I *knew* I shouldn't have told either one of you about the Candy Apple Incident! It wasn't a *freak show*, I said it was a freak *accident*!"

The Candy Apple Incident happened a few months ago when I was shopping and ran into a candy factory. There, in the window, was a shiny green apple wrapped in caramel and then rolled in Oreo cookie bits. It couldn't have been more perfect if my name had been written on it in white chocolate. It was mine, though I decided not to eat it until I got home, so I could savor its beauty in private, where that kind of love belongs.

Heading back to the freeway, I spotted a branch of my bank and decided to deposit a check I had in my purse, so I pulled into the packed drive-thru line and waited. As I was waiting, I looked at the candy apple glistening on the passenger seat. I picked it up by the top of the bag, turned it all the way around, looking at it, admiring it, then tore the cellophane bag off like an animal and sunk my big buck front teeth into it.

And then couldn't get them back out. You see, I had not prepared my toothy lunge with the correct leverage and had plunged my fangs into something of an apple abyss with no way to get them out.

They were stuck.

"Ehhh! Ehhh!" I grunted as I tussled with the apple, trying to pull it down, but not with too much force because my gums bleed already, and I was afraid that instead of ripping my teeth out of the apple, I'd rip my teeth out of my gums instead.

"EH MEH GAAA!" I cried (translation without the candy

apple lodged in my mouth: "Oh my god!") as I struggled, wiggling the candy apple stick to no avail. Then I had an idea. I opened up my jaw as wide as I could, figuring that if I could bite into the apple with my lower teeth, I could scrape up the inside of the apple and free my tusks that way.

I bit in. Hard. As soon as I did, however, I realized I had made a serious mistake when a wave of pain hit me and I understood that I had just pulled a big, fat, uncooperative muscle in both my face and neck and I was temporarily paralyzed.

"AHHHH! AHHHH!" I screamed in agony as I put my foot on the brake and clawed at the apple with both hands. As I wrestled with it, a massive chunk of the apple finally flew off and freed me, but the chunk was so large it wouldn't even fit in my mouth. I tried to chew it as apple juice streamed down my chin, as little bits fell from my chops, and that was when I looked over and found a mother-and-son team staring at me from their white Econoline van in the next lane, their jaws completely dropped in stupor.

What could I do? I just kept chewing and waved.

I adjusted the rearview mirror so I could wipe the juice off, and that's when I saw myself. Smears of cookie crumbs, apple juice, and caramel were all over my face, on my chin, on my nose, on my neck. One smudge almost went all the way to my ear. As I tried to wipe it off with the cellophane bag, I noticed the people in the van again, but this time they were laughing at me. The mom reached up and wiped her eyes.

I decided right then and there that I would avoid a future Candy Apple Incident by carrying a fork and knife with me at all times, and I was trying to tell Jamie and Krysti this as we parked the car in Old Town. They, however, were having none of it.

"No way, Lockjaw," Krysti said. "Who knows what you would do with weapons. You could stick one of us with the knife when we pointed out you had cookie crumbs stuck in your nostrils."

"And stab the other one with a fork when we pointed out that you kind of looked like a barbecued pig with a giant apple stuck in your mouth," Jamie added. "Sometimes I think if a caseworker from social services evaluated you, you could totally qualify for disability."

"Really?" I said, trying hard not to get my hopes up.

We passed the candy apple store, and as Jamie and Krysti waited outside, I went in and got my treat. The candy apple people wrapped it in a pretty cellophane bag and tied it with a ribbon.

It was beautiful. I held it up in the light so that we could all admire its majesty, as I twirled it on the stick to get a full, circular view.

"What's that?" Krysti said as she pointed to an aberration on the apple that seemed to be a big, thick, white fleck of coconut.

"Hmmm," Jamie said, studying it carefully. "Looks like you have some competition. But whoever put on that Candy Apple Freak Show is missing a tooth!"

More Bread, Please

We saw them through the window of the front of the restaurant as we were waiting for a table.

They were glistening, they were steaming, they were slightly browned on top.

They were tiny little rolls swathed in butter and garlic.

Heaven on a platter.

"I can't stop looking at them," I confessed to my friend Jamie as I pressed my face against the glass. "Do you think if I asked the people at that table, they'd give me one?"

"Ask for two," she insisted.

"Excuse me," the hostess said, pointing to us. "You two!"

"Us?" Jamie replied. "Is our table ready?"

"No," she answered sharply. "Stop drooling on that window, you are *scaring* people!"

Being that we were at an ultrahip restaurant in Los Angeles—around the corner from Jamie's new apartment—catering to the ultracool, we were already at a severe disadvantage. Despite the fact that we had bypassed our regular uniform of overalls and hiking boots, we were still slightly underdressed, having left our chunky-heeled, purple suede hip-high boots and turbo breast implants at home. I noticed the difference between "us" and "them" the minute we walked up to the front door.

"Are you sure this is the restaurant?" I asked Jamie as she gave her keys to the valet. "No one here weighs over one hundred pounds. Either this is a casting call for *Scream 15*, or these are the prettiest homeless people I've ever seen."

The hostess, sporting a headset *and* a walkie-talkie, sure was in a hurry to inform us of the hour-and-a-half wait until Jamie mentioned that we had a reservation.

"You can wait over there until your table is ready," she said, pointing outside.

After we shuffled back through the door, I spotted the rolls on the other side of the glass that was the promised land. Then the hostess yelled at us and called our name.

"Follow me," she said as she approached us in her clickety-click chunky shoes.

Jamie and I trailed her meekly to our table and sat down.

"I want rolls," I stated immediately. "Lots and lots of rolls."

BING! As if the Guardian Angel of Hot Breads and Starches had heard my prayer, a little dish with six shiny rolls popped up on our table.

"Six?" Jamie and I exclaimed together. "That's not enough! That's only three apiece! What do we look like, *models*?"

The waiter showed up, sneered at us, then took our order. At the last minute, I decided we absolutely had to have the roasted garlic bulb to accompany the tiny bread delights. I realized it was a silly move once the waiter left, and I was face-to-face with the two surviving rolls on the white plate.

"There's not enough bread for the garlic," Jamie said with wide, panicked eyes. "There is NOT ENOUGH!"

"Don't fear," I said as I waved at a busboy and got his attention. "More bread, please!"

BING! Another white plate appeared on the table, and this time, it was a proverbial MOUNTAIN of rolls. Rolls lining the dish. Rolls piled on top of rolls. Rolls falling off the plate. Rolls tumbling onto the table.

"It's like winning the lottery!" we gasped breathlessly.

Jamie picked one up and popped it into her mouth.

"Don't eat them now!" I cried. "Wait for the garlic!"

"There are thirty of them here," she replied and ate another one.

A second later, the roasted garlic bulb appeared in our waiter's hands—surrounded by thirty more rolls.

He stopped after he placed the new dish on the table and looked at us.

"You got more . . . rolls," he said snootily with a little shake of his head.

We stopped chewing, looked at him, and nodded. In fact, our table was covered now with nothing but plates of rolls.

"Why, it's the Attack of the Carbohydrate Women," he said without a smile as he left.

"He hates us! HURRY!" I hissed, pushing a plate toward Jamie. "We have to eat them all! You take that mound, I'll take this one!"

We were trying to chew really fast, like two chews per roll and swallow, and were halfway done with the second plate of rolls when we noticed that all the waiters that passed by our table were glancing at us and laughing. Some were stopping by just to look at the spectacle. Our waiter came back by to deliver our dinners and asked if he could bring us anything else.

"More bread, please," I said as I chewed, but he didn't think that was very funny.

"He hates us," Jamie confirmed as she ate another roll.

The hostess swung around and handed us a lyric sheet just as Dean Martin began to belt out "That's Amore" over the speakers, which everyone, including the clientele, started singing along to. The waiters, each holding a small glass of wine, took the cue and began toasting people at each table. We watched as our waiter gaily clicked glasses with the folks at the surrounding tables, then the tables in the general vicinity, then with the people far to the front.

"He won't toast with us!" Jamie pouted, holding her glass of iced tea up, just waiting for him to come by and grace us. "He despises us!"

"No," I disagreed. "He LOATHES us."

We spotted him moving back toward the center of the restaurant, laughing and clinking glasses with normal people who were satisfied with one plate of rolls.

The song ended, Jamie sorrowfully put her glass back down on the table, and a busboy immediately filled it back up to the brim.

Suddenly, our waiter was gliding back past our table when he turned, and in an action of complete pity and probably hoping that we might somehow scrounge enough change off the bottom of our purses to give him more than a 10 percent tip, raised his glass toward Jamie and swooped in for the kill.

She quickly fumbled for her glass, and I could see the joy on her face. She, at least, had been redeemed; she was worthy. She had been picked last for the team, but it hardly mattered. She picked up her glass, albeit a little too quickly in her undisguised jubilation. Her iced tea rushed toward his wine with the fury of a speeding train and not understanding the energy and fuel the rolls had provided, she rammed her glass into his with a loud crack as the contents of both exploded and soaked his sleeve and the entire table.

He looked at her, wiped a droplet of iced tea from his chin, and said quietly, "I'll get a towel."

"Oh, don't bother," I said, reaching for one of the numerous white plates on the table. "We'll just use these rolls."

Nothing but a Smile

It was my first real day at the new gym, since I had been black-balled from the community college fitness center when they found out I smoked. Eager to start a new habit that would shrink my butt from a couch to a love seat, I was going to begin exercising. I had just opened my locker and had slapped on the new lock I had bought at Target the day before, when it happened.

She walked by me, then headed toward a bench across the aisle. Standing in front of me was a naked lady, fresh from the shower.

A completely naked lady.

With no clothes on.

I don't even know what my first instinct was. I don't think I had one. All I knew was that a naked lady was standing in front of me, and I was staring at her being naked.

I guess I just couldn't believe it. I had never really seen a naked lady before, except for one time when I was five, and my mom let our hippie neighbor, Honey, take me shopping with her and her five-year-old daughter. Honey took both of us into the dressing room with her, and before I knew what was happening, there was Honey's left "lentil" just hanging there, wide out in the open. I looked at Honey's daughter, who didn't seem too bothered by it, but personally, I was horrified. I was five AND I was a Catholic. The whole thing was just DIRTY. I felt as if I had just witnessed something unholy and shameful, and I never told anyone that filthy secret, not even at confession, until just now. I'm sorry that I kept this from you, Mom, but it's true. I saw Honey's lentil.

I felt dirty then, and I felt dirty now. It was happening all over, but not only were there lentils, there were things my mother never taught me the names of, but then again, I was a little sheltered. Until I was a junior in high school, my mom insisted that the Kotex pads under the bathroom sink were special sponges she used to clean the toilet.

The naked lady, now bending over to dry her legs off, was showing me a whole other view, like her marshmallows.

"Just what is going on here?" is what I wanted to say to the naked lady, because I didn't know this woman. I had no business seeing her NAKED, especially since there was a bathroom stall several feet away. I had no right, and, furthermore, I had no idea when I paid for my gym membership that I had also joined a nudist colony.

Who could be that free? I thought. Who could be that free that they could just strut around "in all candor" in front of other people? Who has that much self-esteem that they could bare it all and not burst into tears? I mean, I have trouble walking from the bath mat to the shower without any clothes on, let alone put on a show for a bunch of strangers. My bra doesn't come off until the sun goes down, and that's the law. I feel perverted if my dog catches a glimpse of me in all my glory, let alone someone I've never even met. When I have to go to the gynecologist, I have to practice sitting on the edge of my bed with no pants on for a week before my appointment, just to get ready.

Obviously, the naked lady had no such problems. I didn't know what to do, and I was so freaked out that I forgot the combination to my new lock. I went home and called my mother.

"You saw a streaker?" my mother said from the other end of the phone. "That is just disgusting. And there was a bathroom stall five feet away? Some people are raised like animals, barnyard animals! They never heard of Sodom and Gomorrah?"

"I don't know," I said, shaking my head.

"When your sister and I joined that gym last year," she continued, "there were so many of them walking around that I just had to stop going. It was like a topless bar! I felt like I should be handing out dollar bills! 'Here's one for you, here's one for you . . .' The last thing I need is to see strangers' lentils! How do I tell that to a priest? You should just stay home and run in place like I do."

Then my sister got on the phone. "Once, when I was in the locker room, I met a friend of mine that owed me money for a lunch, and she wrote me a check right then and there. Completely naked."

"What did you do?" I asked.

"I cashed the check and bought a Tae-Bo videotape," my sister replied. "And I run in place when no one else is home. I can't go to the gym anymore. There's so many naked people around that I feel like I'm in a porno movie. And as for my friend, well . . . I can't eat lunch with someone like that. She can be wearing seven sweaters and a parka, but she'll always be naked to me."

When my boyfriend came home from work that night, he asked me about my first day at the gym, but I told him how the naked lady scared me so badly I had to go home.

"You thought she was dirty, didn't you?" he said.

"Yes," I answered. "Yes, I did."

He just shrugged his shoulders and said, "So? It's a gym, Laurie. People have to take showers. And you're kind of . . . repressed. I can't believe you've never seen a naked lady before."

"Well," I started, "it's not like all of us girls go into the Gap dressing room, take off our clothes, and chase and tickle one another."

"What about your family?" he suggested. "You never saw any of them naked?"

I gasped, sucking in a breath so hard it nearly knocked me backward. "We're a very careful people," I said slowly. "We don't believe in naked!"

"It's very normal to be naked in the locker room," my boyfriend said, trying to calm me. "If you go back, you're probably going to see more naked people."

"Yeah? Well, I'm not playing games with them," I answered. "And I'm not wiping off anybody's back!"

A couple days later, I got up enough courage to go back to the gym. I was getting ready to put my new lock on my locker when I heard an elderly, grandmotherly voice call out to me.

"Dear?" the voice said gently. "Young lady? Could you please help me? I've dropped my comb, and I can't seem to reach it."

"Oh, sure," I said, noticing the comb on the ground.

I picked it up and started to hand it to her, but as I looked up into her sweet little grandmother face, I saw that the only thing she was wearing was a smile.

Special Thanks

I would like to issue a special thanks to my family (yes, Mom, that means you, and Dad, Nana, Lisa, Linda, Taylor, Nicholas, and David) for letting me not only air but spin-cycle all of our dirty laundry out in public and for hardly ever getting mad, even though some of you have threatened to sue me. But remember, I can PROVE IT ALL. Thanks to the ball and chain for letting me say the unthinkable when I needed a punch line, and for not telling his family what I do for a living.

Thanks to Jamie Schroeder-Gomez, Jeff Abbott, Joel Abbott, Nikki Adams, Kate McGinty, Krysti Lindemoen, Patrick Sedillo, Sandra Quijas, Sara Cina, Dionne Gonzales, the Feeney sisters, and all of my friends who let me tell their secrets just so I could make my deadline.

Thanks to Michelle Savoy, Meg Halverson, Bill Hummel, Coni Bourin, Laura Smith, Kathy Murillo, Beth Kawasaki, Eric Searleman, Shamsi and Jamal Ruhe, Jenny Ignaszewski, Sean Fitzpatrick, Troy Fuss, Charlie Levy, Robert Sentinery, Amy Silverman, Theresa Cano, Sarah Wallace, Laura Greenberg, Beth Deveney, Ann Grigsby, Jeff Unger, and my seventh- and ninth-grade English teachers, Mr. Homuth and Mrs. Gaio, for your support and encouragement.

A big thanks to the readers, whom I love and worship for sticking with me longer than any boyfriend did.

A hearty round of applause to all the boys who said they loved me but LIED, which made me a mean, bitter woman. (P.S.: I have lost seventeen pounds after I ate some pork the doctor says was probably way too pink, gotten a lesson in plucking, and learned to apply eyeshadow properly since you last saw me. I haven't gotten my one weird bicuspid fixed yet, but when I get my tax refund this year—and if I don't need new brakes or a D&C—you will no longer be able to call me "Snaggletooth." I am a goddess, and I bet none of you have even made parole yet. So there.)

Oh, yes, and to all of the bosses that fired me from shitty jobs. You know who you are. If I ever have the chance to squeeze another unemployment check out of you or plunder your supply of Post-it Notes, I will briskly seize the opportunity. You have been warned.

With the greatest reverence to Hopkins, who understood everything, who shielded me from the rain on the steps of Tempe Long Wong's so my dress wouldn't get wet, and who taught me the most important, honest things I will ever learn. You may be somewhere in the distance, but you are never out of my sight.

Undying gratitude to the Amazing, Incredible, and Marvelous Jenny Bent, to whom I owe a kidney, both eyes, and the ovary that looks the least gray. She unconditionally rules and is tons better than psychotherapy, even with a really good copay. I can never thank her enough.

Thanks to Nina Graybill for going to bat for me over and over again, and a million American Beauty thank-you's to Pamela Cannon, who took a chance on this supersized dork, and not only because she thought one of my legs was totally shorter than the other. I'm not above embracing pity, so I let her believe it for a minute, but aside from that, she deserves thanks for repeatedly polishing the product of a hunter and pecker, and, EVEN WORSE, a journalism major.

Thank you, thank you, thank you.

And absolutely, I humbly bow to Idiot Girls everywhere.

We simply rock.

Love,

Laurie

ABOUT THE AUTHOR

LAURIE NOTARO has been a humor columnist for ten years. She has been fired from seven jobs (possibly eight) and lives with her first husband and pets (two dogs—a miniature Wookie and a lab that makes doody in her sleep—and a cat with no teeth) in the hot, dry dust bowl of Phoenix, Arizona. *The Idiot Girls' Action-Adventure Club* is her first book. Visit her website at www.laurienotaro.com.

Also by Laurie Notaro

Autobiography of a Fat Bride
TRUE TALES OF A PRETEND ADULTHOOD

Laurie Notaro
Author of the
New York Times bestseller
The Idiot Girls' Action-Adventure Club

[Notaro] dishes out her unique brand of outrageous humor....
A sidesplitting exposé."
—*USA Today*

———

"I love Laurie Notaro.... **She may be the funniest writer in this solar system."**
—*The Miami Herald*

———

"Love Laurie Notaro! Love this book! At a paltry $12.95, this book is worth its weight in gold.... **Don't miss it."**
—New Orleans *Times-Picayune*

In her second collection of essays, Laurie Notaro, leader of the Idiot Girls' Action-Adventure Club, finds grown-up life just as harrowing as her reckless youth, as she meets Mr. Right, moves in, settles down, and crosses the toe-stubbing threshold of matrimony. Life doesn't necessarily get any easier as you get older, but it does get funnier.

VILLARD

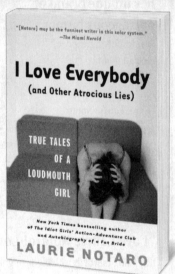